MATT CHRISTOPHER

In the Huddle with....
Steve Young

MATT CHRISTOPHER

In the Huddle with....
Steve Young

Little, Brown and Company
Boston   New York   Toronto   London

First Edition

Library of Congress Cataloging-in-Publication Data

Christopher, Matt.
   Steve Young / Matt Christopher. — 1st ed.
      p. cm.
   Summary: Reviews the life and career of Steve Young, quarterback
for the San Francisco 49ers.
   ISBN 0-316-13793-6 (pb)
   1. Young, Steve, 1961– — Juvenile literature.   2. Football players —
United States — Biography — Juvenile literature.   3. San Francisco 49ers
(Football team) — Juvenile literature. [1. Young, Steve, 1961– .
2. Football players.]   I. Title.
GV939.Y69C57 1996
796.332'092 — dc20
[B]

                                                          96-12553

                   10 9 8 7 6 5 4 3 2 1

                              MV-NY

                   Published simultaneously in Canada
              by Little, Brown & Company (Canada) Limited

                   Printed in the United States of America

To my son Dale

Contents

Chapter One
1961–1980

The Great-Great-Great-Grandson

San Francisco 49er quarterback Steve Young is one of the best pro football players ever. When Young touches the ball, something exciting usually happens. He might drop straight back and pass the ball deep downfield to an open receiver. Or he might scramble around the pocket, then flip the ball to a running back a split second before being sacked. Or he just might fake a pass, stick the ball under his arm, and run downfield like a running back, dodging some tacklers and barreling over others. Whatever he does, the result is usually the same. The 49ers win!

But if you had to pick one word to describe Steve Young, the person, you probably wouldn't use the word *exciting*. For while he is certainly one of the most electrifying quarterbacks in the NFL, football is only a part of his life. Off the field he is quiet and mild-mannered. He lives quietly, plays the piano, and gives generously of his time to a number of charities. In the off-season, he went back to college and became a lawyer.

Perhaps the best word to describe Steve Young, person and quarterback, is *patient*. Young was no overnight sensation. He played football a very, very long time before becoming one of the most exciting players in the history of the National Football League. At every stage of Steve Young's career, from high school and college to professional football, he always started out as a backup to some other player. Yet he never let himself get discouraged. Each time, he remained patient, practiced hard, tried to help his team, and waited for his opportunity to play. When he finally got his chance, he played as well as he could. Over and over, that strategy earned Young the starting quarterback position on each team he played for and allowed him to achieve his goals in life — including the biggest goal in football, winning the Super Bowl.

Patience and perseverance are something of a trademark in the Young family. They don't give up easily. Steve's great-great-great-grandfather Brigham Young was a pioneer in the American West. As president of the Church of Jesus Christ of Latter Day Saints, or Mormons, Brigham Young helped lead a group of Mormon settlers from the East and Midwest all the way across North America. They settled in what eventually became the state of Utah.

At first, life was hard for the pioneers. Utah was high desert country. It was hot and very dry in the summer, and cold and snowy in the winter. No one thought the Mormons could survive in such an inhospitable environment. But Brigham Young and his followers didn't give up. They learned to irrigate the land and grow crops in the desert. More and more people moved to Utah. In 1896, nineteen years after Young's death, Utah became the forty-fifth state.

Steve's father, LeGrande Young, was born and raised in Utah. As a young boy, LeGrande earned the nickname "Grit," because he was so strong and tough.

Grit Young was also a pretty good football player. He went to Brigham Young University, a college named after his great-great-grandfather, and played running back on the football team. Although the team wasn't very successful, Grit Young was the Cougars' best player.

After he graduated, Grit Young became engaged to and married a classmate, Sherry Steed. He then started studying for a degree in law at the University of Utah.

Grit was still in law school when his first son, Jon Steven Young, was born on October 11, 1961. The young couple called their son plain old Steve. Two years later, they had another son, Michael. Eventually the Youngs had three more children, two boys, named Tom and Jimmy, and a daughter, Melissa.

After Grit graduated from law school in 1964, the Young family moved to Lone Park, a small suburb of Salt Lake City, the Utah state capital. Grit entered the business world and was hired by a large corporation.

In Lone Park, Steve and Michael found plenty of playmates. Whenever they had a chance, they were out in the yard, playing some kind of game.

Even when he was a little boy, Steve was a good

4

athlete. At age two he could do push-ups. At three he learned to dribble a basketball. When he went out to play, Steve usually sought the company of older boys while little Mike trailed behind.

In 1969, Grit Young was transferred by his company to New York City. The entire family piled into their station wagon and headed east, retracing the route that Brigham Young had taken more than one hundred years before. Grit and Sherry Young bought a house in Greenwich, Connecticut, a suburb of New York City.

Steve went into third grade at North Mianus Elementary School. Like many of his classmates, he loved sports. Whenever his teachers would assign a report, Steve would write about sports. After school, he played midget baseball, basketball, and football. He liked football best.

At first Steve played wide receiver, but before too long he was switched to quarterback. Steve was thrilled. His favorite team was the Dallas Cowboys, and their quarterback, Roger Staubach, was his hero. Steve tried to act just like Staubach, although because he was left-handed, he had to do some things differently from the way the right-handed

Cowboy did them. With Steve at quarterback, his team won the league championship.

After elementary school, Steve attended Eastern Junior High. He tried out for the football team and was named starting quarterback.

Although Steve was a good player, he wasn't a star. The offense had only a few passing plays, so Steve usually handed off or ran the ball himself.

At the end of one season, Eastern faced arch rival Darien for the league championship. With only seconds left to play, Eastern trailed by a few points but had the ball on the one-yard line. A touchdown would win the game.

The coach sent in a play. Steve was supposed to hand the ball off to the fullback, who would run off-tackle. Eastern lined up at the line of scrimmage, sure they would soon be celebrating a victory. But at the last second, Steve decided he would try to score the touchdown himself.

The center snapped him the ball, and Steve tried to sneak over the goal line. When everyone got untangled, Steve was inches short of the goal. Eastern lost the game.

"What happened?" the coach yelled at Steve after the game. "You were supposed to hand the ball off!"

"I thought I could make it," answered thirteen-year-old Steve sheepishly. The coach just shook his head. It was hard to stay angry at Steve. He was just trying to win.

There was also more to Steve Young's life than sports. Each Sunday, Steve and his younger brothers and sister rose at five A.M. and traveled thirty miles to attend day-long Mormon religion classes. Each weekday, they awoke at the same time to attend shorter classes before school. Once Steve got to school, he was a straight-A student, well liked by both his classmates and his teachers. Steve's example left an impression on the other Young children. His brother Mike, who later became a doctor, once told a reporter, "I owe a lot of what I am to Steve. He wanted everything to be right, so he did everything right. I was able to see the success he had, and it made me want to do that also."

By the time Steve entered Greenwich High School to begin tenth grade, he was one of the best athletes in his class. But no one expected him to be a star. There were lots of good athletes at Greenwich High.

In Steve's sophomore year, he didn't even make the varsity football team. He played quarterback for the junior varsity, and the team finished with a miserable 1–10 record.

Although he made the varsity team the following year, and was even named co-captain by coach Mike Ornato, Steve Young didn't expect to play much as a junior. Senior quarterback Bill Barber led the Greenwich Cardinals' offense. Steve was only a second-string player.

Still, Steve worked hard in practice. The Cardinals ran the "wishbone" offense, which took a long time to learn to run properly. In the wishbone, each play starts out looking the same, and the quarterback has to decide from among a number of options what to do. He can either hand the ball off, pitch it to a running back, keep the ball himself, or, once in a while, roll out and throw a pass.

Even though he didn't expect to play much, Steve concentrated on mastering the wishbone. He might not get a chance to play as a junior, but he still had his senior year ahead of him. He would just have to be patient.

But just before the season opened, Barber hurt

his shoulder. All of a sudden, Steve Young was the starting quarterback!

In his first varsity game, against Ridgefield, Steve ran the wishbone to perfection. In the first quarter he led the Cardinals downfield to the ten-yard line. When he took the snap, he faked to the fullback and started sprinting down the line. His halfback trailed behind.

Just as Steve was ready to turn the corner, a defensive player came up to make the tackle. But Steve faked a pitch to his halfback. The defensive player hesitated, and Steve cut toward the goal line. Touchdown! Greenwich led 7–0.

Late in the game, with the score 21–0, Steve got a chance to try out his throwing arm. With the Cardinals on the 21-yard line, Coach Ornato decided to cross up the defense and pass the ball. Steve faded back and spotted a receiver, Greg Campbell, wide open in the end zone. He reared back and threw.

The ball sailed toward Campbell in a wobbly spiral. At the last second Campbell dove, stretched out, and caught the ball, pulling it to his chest as he hit the ground. It was Steve Young's first high school touchdown pass! The Cardinals won, 27–0.

Steve Young played so well that poor Bill Barber never got back into the lineup. With Steve at quarterback, the Cardinals finished the season 7–2.

Steve matched his strong performance on the football field with similarly satisfying seasons in basketball and baseball. He was selected by his teammates as co-captain of each team and made the starting lineup. On the basketball team, he played guard. Against Stamford High, he scored 17 points. On the baseball diamond, Steve played center field and pitcher. He won three games as a southpaw hurler.

By the time his senior year approached, big things were expected from Steve Young. His surprising performance as a junior had made everyone realize that he was one of the best quarterbacks in the state. Greenwich fans expected Young to lead the team to the league championship.

Coach Ornato wanted to take advantage of both Steve's running and passing ability. In the offseason, he abandoned the wishbone offense for the "veer." The veer offense isn't quite as run-oriented as the wishbone.

In the first game of the season, the Cardinals got off to a fast start, winning 48–21. Steve Young was magnificent, running the ball 14 times for 129 yards and scoring two touchdowns.

Over the next two months, the Cardinals rolled over their opponents, losing only twice, including one game that Steve had to sit out with a sore shoulder. With each win, Steve received more and more credit and became more popular with his teammates and classmates. Sometimes his popularity put him in awkward situations.

After each game, Steve's teammates often gathered for big parties. Even though they were under age and knew it was wrong, someone usually brought beer to the party.

The first time one of his teammates offered Steve Young a beer, he politely refused. When they asked again, Steve explained that the use of alcohol was against his religion. As a Mormon, he was forbidden to use alcohol, caffeine, or tobacco.

"Come on," one of his teammates pleaded. "You have to have a drink of something with us!"

"Well," said Steve, "do you have any milk?"

Steve's teammates started to laugh, and then they realized that Steve was serious. They raced into the kitchen and came back with a bottle of milk. Steve raised it to his lips, and his teammates all applauded. After that, whenever Steve Young attended a party at Greenwich, someone always made sure there was a bottle of milk in the refrigerator for him.

Steve Young played the best game of his high school career against the Stamford Catholic Crusaders. The Crusaders were led by quarterback Roger Haggerty. The game was touted as a matchup between the two best quarterbacks in the state. By the end of the game, there was no doubt who was the better of the two.

On only the fifth play of the game, Steve broke free on the option play and raced 52 yards for a touchdown. Then he led the Cardinals on a 96-yard drive, dashing the final 22 yards himself to make the score 14–0.

But the Crusaders, and their quarterback, refused to quit. Stamford scored the next 27 points and led Greenwich 27–14 as the game entered the third quarter. Then Steve Young went to work.

First he led the team on a 69-yard touchdown march, closing the score to 27–20. The Cardinals failed to make the extra point, but on their next possession, Steve drove them inside the Crusader ten. Although Greenwich lost the ball on downs, Stamford immediately fumbled. The Cardinals took full advantage of the turnover and scored again. They tried to take the lead with a two-point conversion, but Steve was stopped short. Stamford still led, 27–26, with less than two minutes left in the game.

Coach Ornato called for an onside kick. The Greenwich kicking team swarmed onto the ball. Steve Young and the Cardinal offense had one more chance.

The Cardinals worked the ball to the Stamford 35-yard line. But time was running out. There were only seconds left to play.

Steve Young dropped back as Greg Campbell, his favorite receiver, raced downfield. Steve reached his arm back and flung the ball into the end zone.

Campbell and the Crusader defender both went up for the ball. Both reached out and wrapped their arms around it. As they fell to the ground, each player had his hands on the ball.

But as Campbell hit the ground, he managed to pull the ball free. The referee hesitated for a second until he was sure Campbell had the ball. Then his hands shot into the air. Touchdown, Greenwich! The Cardinals won, 32–27!

College scouts began flocking to Greenwich High football games to catch a glimpse of the young quarterback. As impressed as they were with Steve's leadership and running ability, his passing arm did not excite anyone. Most of the scouts thought Young should change positions in college and play either running back or defensive back. Against Rippowam High, Coach Ornato tried to help Steve's chances to impress the scout and had him play running back at times. Steve ran for more than a hundred yards and Greenwich won, 27–0.

The victory meant that Greenwich earned the right to play arch rival Darien on Thanksgiving Day for the Fairfield County Interscholastic Athletic Conference championship.

More than ten thousand fans turned out for the game, the last football game of Steve Young's high school career. Steve hoped to end the season with a victory.

Darien focused their entire defense on the Cardinal quarterback. Everywhere Steve went, two or three defenders went right with him. Although

Steve still managed to rush for 117 yards on 21 carries, he completed only 5 of 15 passes for 58 yards and was unable to lead the Cardinals over the goal line. Darien won, 17–0.

No one was more disappointed by the loss than Steve. Still, he felt good about his high school career. In his two years at the helm of the Cardinal varsity, he had completed more than 40 percent of his passes for 1,220 yards, and he rushed for 1,928 yards, second best in school history.

Now that football season was over, the most important question in Steve Young's life became where he would attend college. Colleges were eager to have him on campus. Few freshman candidates could match his academic and athletic performance in high school. Cornell, Virginia, Syracuse, and North Carolina were among the colleges that offered him a football scholarship.

As attractive as these offers were, Steve was disappointed. There was only one college he wanted to attend: Brigham Young University, the school named after his great-great-great-grandfather. BYU's football program was top-notch and beginning to gain a national reputation.

But there was only one problem. BYU didn't even try to recruit players from the East Coast. No one at BYU had ever heard of Steve Young.

Then Steve got lucky. One of Grit Young's friends was a close friend of BYU head coach LaVell Edwards. He contacted the coach and put in a good word for Steve. BYU already had too many quarterbacks, but as a favor to his friend, Edwards reviewed Steve's academic and athletic record. He liked what he saw — and offered Steve a scholarship. Steve was ecstatic.

It seemed to him as if the rest of his high school career passed in a blur. Every day, he woke up, went to church, attended school, practiced with either the basketball or baseball teams, came home, did his homework, went out with his friends for an hour or so, then went to bed, and got up at five A.M. ready to do it all again. Along the way, he still averaged nearly 15 points per game on the basketball team, with a high of 24 against Ridgefield, made the Honor Society, won an English award, hit .400 for the baseball team, and pitched a no-hitter against New Canaan. On June 7, the day after his senior prom, Steve pitched another no-hitter in the

Greenwich Senior Babe Ruth League. The dedicated milk drinker was about the only player on the field who was not hung over.

High school was over. Steve Young had accomplished just about everything there was to accomplish. He was ready to move on.

Under his picture in his high school yearbook, Steve Young described his ambitions as "to enjoy victory and grow stronger with defeat." Those words were prophetic. Over the next few seasons, he would have the opportunity to do both.

Eighth String to Starter

Steve Young arrived at Brigham Young University in August of 1980 full of confidence and optimism about the future. In high school, he had overcome every challenge to become the best quarterback in the state of Connecticut. He expected to have the same success at BYU.

Although Steve Young's desire to attend BYU was certainly understandable, BYU was not the best place for him to be playing football. The BYU Cougars played a style of football much different from that played by the Greenwich High Cardinals. Under Coach LaVell Edwards, BYU was a passing team. In their potent, high-scoring offense, BYU quarterbacks sometimes threw the ball fifty times a game. Former BYU quarterbacks Gifford Nielson and Marc Wilson were already stars in the NFL, and current quarterback Jim McMahon was setting new records every game. Sportswriters were beginning to call BYU "Quarterback U." Based on his performance in high school, it did not appear that Steve Young threw the ball well enough to play quarterback for BYU.

As soon as Steve had settled into his dorm room, he raced over to the football office to check in with the coaches and find out when practice started. On a bulletin board, the BYU coaching staff had posted lists that included all players, their positions, and, in descending order, where they were ranked with other players at their position.

Steve eagerly scanned the chart until he found the list with the heading QUARTERBACKS. Then he looked for his name.

BYU star Jim McMahon was first. After McMahon was backup quarterback Royce Bybee, then third-string quarterback Eric Krzmarzick.

Steve kept going down the list. He finally found his name way at the bottom. He was the eighth-string quarterback!

Steve was crushed. He had known he would face an uphill battle at BYU, but he never dreamed he would be eighth string. When practice started, he didn't even get to try out for the varsity. Instead, he was assigned to the junior varsity team. BYU quarterback coach Doug Scovil didn't think much of Young, and told him so. Even on the JV squad, Young was a third stringer.

Steve tried to be patient and stay optimistic. At practice, he worked hard on his passing and tried to absorb the complicated BYU offense. When practice was over, he spent most of his time studying and rarely left his room. The high school star was more than a little overwhelmed by college life.

In his first few weeks at BYU, Steve was depressed and homesick. He didn't even bother to unpack most of his bags. Nearly every day, he called home.

He felt a little better when the JV season began. Although Steve wasn't in the starting lineup, he did get to play a little bit in every game. When Steve was on the field, JV coach Lance Reynolds usually changed his offense from the usual BYU passing style to a running offense. Steve was successful with this style, but running the football did little to prepare him to head the varsity offense.

While Steve languished on the JV team, the varsity, led by junior quarterback Jim McMahon, was playing some of the best football in the country. Steve stood little chance of proving himself.

Then, halfway through the season, he finally got a break. The varsity was scheduled to play Wyoming, which used the wishbone. Because Steve had experience with that offense, he was asked to run the "scout" team, the team that practiced against BYU's starting defense the week before the game.

Steve shone all week and ran the scout team with ease. Even BYU coach LaVell Edwards took notice of his performance.

When the varsity took the field against Wyoming, Steve Young and the JVs traveled to play the University of Nevada at Las Vegas (UNLV). JV coach Reynolds let Steve run the wishbone, and he took the squad in for a touchdown on their first possession. But when Reynolds eventually replaced him with first one, then the other two JV quarterbacks, they started passing the ball and played even better than Steve had. He was almost right back where he started.

The varsity went undefeated in the regular season and was selected to play in the Holiday Bowl in

San Diego, California, against Southern Methodist University. Based on his earlier performance on the scout team, Steve was now selected to imitate SMU quarterback Lance McIlhenny. As a reward for his hard work, he was allowed to travel with the team to San Diego and to dress for the game.

Steve had performed his job to perfection, but no amount of practice could have prepared the BYU defense for SMU. As Steve stood on the sidelines and watched, SMU obliterated BYU. With only four minutes left to play, BYU trailed 45–25.

But BYU quarterback Jim McMahon deserved his reputation as the best college quarterback in the country. As Steve looked on in wonder, McMahon led the Cougars to three touchdowns in the final four minutes, including a final scoring strike of 46 yards on the last play of the game. Incredibly, BYU won, 46–45.

Although Steve was pleased with the Cougar win, he was still unhappy with BYU. The final blow came when the coaching staff asked him to consider playing defensive back.

After the Holiday Bowl, Steve couldn't wait to get home for winter break. He wanted to ask his father a question.

A few days after arriving home, Steve finally mustered the courage to speak honestly with his father. He told Grit Young that he was miserable at BYU. "Dad," said Steve, "I've had it with the whole thing. I'm not having fun. I think I'm going to quit. Can I come back home?"

Grit Young was silent. He knew that his son was unhappy living thousands of miles away from home, but he also knew that no one in his family had ever quit anything before. After all, if old Brigham Young had quit, there wouldn't ever have been a Brigham Young University.

"Steve," said Grit to his son, "you can quit. But if you quit, you can't come home. There are no quitters here." Steve returned to BYU after break.

It was a difficult thing to do, but Steve Young's decision to give BYU another try couldn't have been wiser or more perfectly timed. At the end of the year, quarterback coach Doug Scovil quit and was replaced by Ted Tollner. Tollner's arrival made all the difference in the world for Steve.

Whereas Scovil had looked at Steve and seen a defensive back, Tollner looked at him and saw the heir apparent to Jim McMahon. Steve had spent hours practicing passing, and he was beginning to throw the ball with authority. At spring practice, Tollner made it clear that he was grooming Steve Young as McMahon's replacement. All of a sudden, Steve was the second-string quarterback. His patience — and that push from his father — were paying off. Things were looking up.

All summer long, Steve worked hard to stay in shape. That fall, Jim McMahon and the Cougars picked up where they had left off the season before. Behind McMahon's golden right arm, the Cougars rolled through the first month of the 1981 season.

In most games, with BYU way ahead, Steve got to play the last quarter. In a 65–8 pasting of the University of Texas at El Paso, he threw his first varsity touchdown pass. Although Steve was glad to play and knew he was improving, he also knew that no matter what he did, he wasn't going to beat out Jim McMahon. McMahon, a senior, was simply too important to sideline in favor of an unproven sophomore. Steve would just have to remain patient and keep working hard.

It was a good thing he did. In the fourth game of the season, with the Cougars leading Colorado 17–0,

McMahon faded back to pass and was hit just as he released the ball. He crumpled to the ground and was carried off the field with a badly sprained knee.

As Steve started quickly warming up, Coach Tollner put an arm around his shoulder. "Steve," he said, "you're the man now." Steve nodded and trotted into the game.

On the first play, Steve completed a pass for 27 yards. Then he faded back again, saw all his receivers covered, and scrambled for a 29-yard gain. Two plays later he tossed an 11-yard touchdown pass. It had taken a grand total of forty-nine seconds for Steve to move the Cougars in for a score!

BYU rolled to a 44–20 win. While McMahon healed, Steve Young became the Cougars' number one quarterback.

He didn't disappoint. With BYU's 17-game winning streak on the line against Utah State, Steve led the Cougars to a comeback win, completing 21 of 40 passes for over 300 yards. After the game, BYU was ranked eighth in the nation, the highest in the school's history.

One week later, the winning streak ended. Steve Young started at quarterback for the Cougars that day, but it probably wouldn't have mattered who played quarterback for BYU; UNLV couldn't be stopped. Although Steve threw four interceptions, he also led the Cougars to 41 points. But the Rebels of UNLV gained more than 600 yards on offense and scored 45 points.

His knee finally healed, McMahon returned to the lineup a week later. Over the final six games of the season, Steve Young barely played. He finished the year completing 55 of 112 passes for 731 yards and five touchdowns. Not Jim McMahon numbers, but with McMahon graduating to the NFL, they were good enough to ensure that Steve Young would be the starting quarterback for the 1982 season.

Steve worked hard in the off-season. He wanted to make sure that he understood the BYU offense and that he was in good physical condition. Everyone expected him to pick right up where McMahon had left off.

In the season opener against UNLV, he did. The Cougars gained revenge for their loss a year before, shutting down the Rebels as Steve completed 73 percent of his passes, threw for one touchdown, and ran for another.

For the second game of the season, the Cougars traveled to Georgia to play the sixth-ranked Bulldogs. Steve Young faced the toughest test of his young career.

In the first half, the BYU defense played great and nearly shut down the powerful Georgia offense. But the BYU offense struggled. Steve threw five interceptions. At halftime, the score was tied 7–7.

Despite the interceptions, Steve still came out throwing in the second half. When he completed a 21-yard touchdown pass to wide receiver Scott Collie, BYU led 14–7.

But Georgia surged back. BYU's defense finally wore down, and the Bulldogs scored ten unanswered points to go ahead 17–14. Then, in the game's last minute, Steve threw his sixth interception. BYU lost.

After the game, Cougar fans wondered if Steve Young was the right man to be playing quarterback for BYU. His poor performance had squandered a fine effort by the BYU defense. A week later, although Steve played better, BYU lost again, this time to Air Force, 39–38. Cougar fans began to grow impatient. After all, in the five games featuring Steve as starting quarterback, the Cougars were 2–3.

But Steve Young didn't share the fans' impatience. He knew that he just had to keep working hard and remain patient himself. Interceptions are usually the result of impatience. The quarterback who doesn't wait long enough usually tries to force the ball to a receiver who isn't open yet. Young told himself to slow down and take his time.

The strategy worked. One week later, against the University of Texas at El Paso, he passed for 399 yards, ran for nearly 100 more, and led BYU to a big win. When a winning streak followed, Steve Young was on his way. No one at BYU ever questioned his ability again.

Late in the season, BYU faced San Diego State. San Diego was coached by Doug Scovil, the former BYU quarterback coach who had wanted to make Steve Young a defensive back. Steve Young wanted to beat San Diego State very badly.

Steve made Scovil wish he *had* made him a defensive back. The Cougars crushed San Diego 58–8 as the BYU quarterback turned in one of the best performances of his career, running for two touchdowns and nearly 100 yards and throwing two touch-down passes. One week later, when BYU beat Utah, they earned the right to play Ohio State in the 1981 Holiday Bowl.

What a difference two years had made! As a fresh-man, Young had stood on the sidelines during the Holiday Bowl without any hope of playing. As a sophomore, he warmed the bench again as he played backup to McMahon. But now, as a junior, he was leading the Cougars against powerful Ohio State, one of the best teams in the country!

Although Steve Young was equal to his task, his teammates were not. Ohio State controlled the foot-ball and marched up and down the field at will. When BYU had the ball, Steve did all he could, com-pleting 27 passes and throwing for two touchdowns, but he didn't get much help. Ohio State won, 40–17.

Still, it had been a satisfying year for Steve Young. He was named conference Player of the Year and earned an honorable mention on several All-American teams. Even better, he wasn't homesick as much anymore. The university named for his great-great-great-grandfather felt like home.

Chapter Three
1982-1984

The Star

Although Steve was happier at BYU, he still missed his parents and the rest of his family. During spring break of his junior year, Steve and two friends from BYU, Jill Simmons and Eric Hunn, piled into Simmons's car and set off on the long drive back east to visit their families.

The three students planned to drive almost non-stop, switching drivers whenever someone got sleepy. Steve took the first shift and drove all night until the trio reached Nebraska. Then Steve traded positions with Jill Simmons.

As soon as Jill started driving, Steve fell asleep. Moments later, he woke with a start. The car was drifting off the road!

Steve looked over and saw his friend slumped over in her seat. He tried to wake her, but she failed to respond. At the last second Steve grabbed the wheel and tried to steer the car to safety.

He was too late. The car was out of control. It ran off the highway and flipped over and over and over.

When the car finally stopped rolling, Steve and Eric were stunned, yet except for a few cuts and scratches, neither was badly hurt. But Jill Simmons was dead.

The tragedy shook Steve badly. While the accident wasn't his fault, he still blamed himself for not being behind the wheel and for not waking up earlier. He even blamed himself for attending BYU. If he had gone to some other school, he reasoned, his friend might still be alive.

Throughout the spring and summer, Steve tried to cope with his feelings. But when he began his senior year, he was full of self-doubt. At the same time, he faced greater pressures than ever before. Although BYU had to rebuild its entire offensive line, everyone still expected Steve Young to blossom into one of the best quarterbacks in the country. BYU fans expected another conference championship and trip to the Holiday Bowl.

All Steve could do was work hard and be patient,

both with himself and with his less experienced teammates. If life had taught him anything, it was that eventually everything would work out okay.

In the 1982 season opener, BYU faced Baylor University. Steve picked up right where he had left off the year before, throwing for 351 yards and running for 113 more. But BYU's 36 points were not enough. Baylor scored 40, and the Cougars lost.

Yet somehow the defeat restored Steve's confidence. He had done well, and knew he could do even better. On the plane ride back to Utah, he overheard some of his teammates blame the BYU coaching staff for the defeat.

Steve got out of his seat and went over to his teammates. He looked them straight in the eye and said, "Don't worry. We won't lose another game the rest of the year." He meant it.

The next week against Bowling Green, Steve made good on his promise. He threw for five touchdowns and 384 yards, then added two more scores on the ground. Steve personally accounted for seven of BYU's nine touchdowns. The Cougars crushed Bowling Green 63–28.

His performance drew headlines all around the

country. Steve Young was becoming famous. He followed by throwing for an amazing 486 yards against Air Force in a 46–28 win a week later. Through the first three games of the season, Young had thrown for over 1,200 yards, with nine touchdowns and only one meaningless interception. Sportswriters began mentioning his name as a candidate for the Heisman Trophy.

The Heisman Trophy is awarded each season by the Downtown Athletic Club of New York City and is based on a vote of sportswriters. Although any college player is eligible to win, it is usually given to a quarterback or running back.

No player from the Western Athletic Conference, not even Jim McMahon, had ever won the award. Most voters were from the Midwest, South, and East Coast, and they tended to vote for players from their own part of the country. For Steve Young to win, he would have to impress voters everywhere.

In his first test, against UCLA at the Rose Bowl in California, he stumbled. BYU managed a win, 37–35, but Steve was outplayed by UCLA quarterback Steve Bono.

Yet after that, nothing, no one, and no team could

stop Steve Young. He led BYU to big wins over Wyoming and New Mexico, passing for more than 340 yards in each game. Then he got another chance to prove himself against San Diego State and his former coach Doug Scovil.

Steve was even better than he had been the year before. He torched Scovil's team for 446 yards and three touchdowns, completing 32 of 45 passes.

But no matter how well he did, some BYU fans still compared him to Jim McMahon. McMahon, they thought, was the tougher quarterback. They felt that Steve was still untested and wondered how he would react to adversity. A week later, against Utah State, Steve was able to silence those who questioned his toughness.

Early in the first quarter, he was blindsided and took a hard hit. He began to play poorly, and the BYU coaches pulled him from the game.

Second-string quarterback Robbie Bosco played well in Steve's absence, but with only minutes left to play, BYU trailed 34–31.

Enter Steve Young. After convincing the team doctor he was okay, he expertly marched the Cougars down the field as the clock ran down. With only eleven seconds remaining, Steve proved just how tough he was. Instead of passing for the score, he simply put his head down and bulled his way over the goal from the one-yard line. BYU won again, 38–34.

As BYU kept winning, and Steve continued to play well, he received more credit and more attention. Nearly every week, a magazine writer flew into Provo to do a feature on him, and he was making so many television appearances that his teammates joked that he should have his own program.

But Steve Young refused to allow his fame to go to his head. He still drove around in his beat-up 1965 Oldsmobile with more than two hundred thousand miles on it, the only car he could afford. For fun, Steve liked to play golf or hang out at a local water slide. Whenever he was asked, he made appearances for charity and spoke to groups of children. He was more than just an All-American player. Steve Young was an All-American person.

Over the last three games of the season, Steve exceeded even his own high standards. Against UT–El Paso, he completed 30 of 43 passes for 359 yards and three touchdowns. Against Colorado State, he completed 33 of 45 passes for 311 yards and two touchdowns. As he had promised, BYU just kept winning.

In his final regular season game for BYU, the Cougars faced arch rival Utah in Provo. For many BYU fans, it would be the last time they would have a chance to see Steve Young play.

A record crowd packed the stadium to bid Steve farewell. In front of his "home" crowd, Steve wanted to play the best football of his career.

Twenty-five times he dropped back to pass. Twenty-two times he put the ball right in his receiver's arms, a completion rate of 88 percent, the best of his collegiate career. He also threw six touchdown passes, another career high. BYU won, 55–7.

The big win provided an exclamation point to a remarkable season. While leading BYU to a 10–1 record and top ten ranking, Steve had virtually rewritten the college record book for passing. His 306 completions for the season, 71.3 completion percentage, and average of 395.1 yards of total offense (passing yards plus rushing yards) per game set NCAA records.

Steve Young was a consensus All-American. Better yet, he did almost as well in the classroom, where he studied international relations and finance. Steve was one of only eleven players in the nation selected by the National Football Hall of Fame to receive a scholar-athlete scholarship.

All that was left for Steve Young to win was the Heisman Trophy and the Holiday Bowl. On December 1, he flew to New York for the Heisman ceremony.

Although Steve played remarkably well all year, running back Mike Rozier of Nebraska was still the heavy favorite to win the award. Steve was so certain Rozier would win that he didn't even prepare a speech.

Steve was right. Rozier won, collecting 1,801 points, while Steve finished second, with 1,172 points. That was still the highest finish any player from the Western Area Conference, and BYU, had ever had.

As soon as the ceremony was over, Steve Young and the BYU Cougars began preparing for the Holiday Bowl game against the Missouri Tigers. Steve hoped to cap off his collegiate career with play equal to his performance against Utah in the regular season finale.

But the month-long break between the end of the regular season and the Bowl game took a toll on the team, and especially its quarterback. During that time, Steve traveled the country receiving awards. The precise timing of the Cougar passing offense suffered.

In the first half of the Holiday Bowl, Steve Young played some of the worst football of his career. He completed only 9 of 17 passes and threw three interceptions.

Steve played much better in the second half, but with less than five minutes left to play, Missouri led, 17–14. The Cougars, and Steve Young, had one more chance. BYU took over on the seven-yard line. Victory was 93 long yards away.

Steve quickly moved the ball down the field on a 53-yard pass play. But a few plays later, he fumbled. BYU recovered the ball, yet time was running out. Two plays later and it was third down. Only thirty seconds remained in the game.

BYU was desperate. They knew that Missouri expected Steve to pass and would be ready for it. So the BYU coaches decided to use a special, trick play, one they'd never tried in a game before.

When Steve got the play from the sidelines, he thought for a second, then smiled faintly. It just might work, he said to himself.

Steve stood behind the center and barked out the signals. The Missouri defense dug in. Steve Young took the snap.

He spun around, took a few steps back, then handed the ball off to Cougar halfback Eddie Stinnett. Stinnett took the ball and followed the big BYU offensive line around the right side on a sweep. Steve Young nonchalantly trotted the opposite way, watching the play.

The Missouri defense hesitated for a second, making sure Steve had actually handed the ball off, then raced after Stinnett. That was exactly what BYU was waiting for.

Steve had to remain patient as he looked back over his shoulder and watched the play develop. He had to make sure he didn't give it away too soon.

Stinnett suddenly stopped in his tracks and looked back to his left, toward Steve. Steve, the best passer in college football, started running hard upfield in the flat as a receiver!

Stinnett lofted a wobbly spiral in the quarterback's direction. Steve stretched out, caught the ball, and headed for the goal line.

Now Steve Young turned into a running back. All that time spent running the wishbone at Greenwich High, running the scout team at BYU, and biding his time, being patient, was about to pay off.

As Steve neared the goal line, he had one BYU blocker ahead of him. One Missouri defender stood in his path.

Instead of blasting his way straight to the goal line, Steve patiently waited until the defensive player made his move to go around the blocker. Then Steve slowed, nimbly stepped to the side, and cut against the grain behind his blocker.

The Missouri tackler tried to reach past the blocker and grab hold of Steve, but his hands grasped only air. Steve Young dashed into the end zone.

Touchdown! Steve jumped up and down and hugged his teammates. BYU had won, 21–14!

Four years before, Young had started his collegiate career as an eighth-string backup quarterback. Now in the last play of his last college game, he had proven that he was not only a great quarterback but a pretty good receiver and running back, too. In college football, there didn't seem to be anything on the field that Steve Young couldn't do.

He would soon find out if that were true in professional football as well.

Chapter Four
1984–1985

The Forty-Million-Dollar Man

When Steve Young allowed himself to dream, he dreamed of a career in the National Football League. Ever since he had watched quarterback Roger Staubach lead the Dallas Cowboys, he had wanted to become an NFL quarterback. Now it seemed as if his dream was destined to come true. Pro scouts were excited about him.

But the National Football League wasn't the only league interested in him. In 1983, the United States Football League, or USFL, was formed. Unlike the NFL, the USFL played football in the spring and summer. The new league hoped eventually to become either as big as the NFL or to force the NFL to merge with it, much the same way as the old American Football League had merged with the NFL in 1970.

There was only one way for the USFL to achieve its goals. The USFL had to attract fans. The only way to do that was to have great players.

Weeks before their draft, the USFL sent a representative to ask Steve Young if he would consider an offer from the new league.

Although Steve was more interested in the NFL, he knew that the USFL was paying some players incredible salaries, worth millions of dollars more than the NFL. After thinking for a moment Steve answered simply, "I'll talk."

The Los Angeles Express of the USFL wanted Steve Young. A year before, they had tried to sign Pittsburgh quarterback Dan Marino, only to have Marino sign with the NFL Miami Dolphins and become a star.

But there was only one problem. The Express, who had finished the 1983 season 8–10, had the eleventh pick of the USFL draft.

Express owner William Oldenburg, aware of how important it was to the league to have a successful team in Los Angeles, asked the other league owners not to draft Steve Young. They agreed.

On January 4, 1984, Steve Young was selected by

the Los Angeles Express in the USFL draft. Then things got complicated.

The USFL season started in late February. The NFL draft wasn't until May. Steve and his agent, Leigh Steinberg, had to make a decision. Did he sign with the USFL or wait for the NFL draft?

They discussed their options. If Steve signed with the USFL, he would probably become the starting quarterback for a team in one of the biggest cities in the country. He had the opportunity to help make the USFL the equal of the NFL.

But if Steve decided to wait for the NFL draft, he'd have a chance to fulfill his childhood dream. The Cincinnati Bengals, with the first pick in the draft, told him they planned to draft him. But they also said that he would have to back up veteran quarterback Ken Anderson for a few years before taking over. As he later told one reporter, "Who knows if I'd get a chance for three or four years?"

Steve didn't like the idea of sitting on the bench. And Los Angeles was a lot closer to Utah than Cincinnati was. Still, playing in the USFL was risky. What if the new league failed?

Los Angeles did all it could to convince Steve to

play in the USFL. They drafted his BYU teammate and best friend, tight end Gordon Hudson. Then they brought in highly respected coach Sid Gillman as an assistant. Gillman had helped develop some of the greatest quarterbacks in football history.

There was also the question of money. In the past year, several NFL quarterbacks had signed for about one million dollars a year. The Bengals told Steve Young and his agent that their best offer was a five-year contract worth 3.5 million dollars.

That was a lot money, but the Express promised even more. They wanted Steve Young badly and were willing to do just about anything to get him.

Negotiations stretched through February and into March. The USFL season had already started, and the Express lost their first two games. Worse, only ten thousand fans bothered to show up for their last game.

Then team owner William Oldenburg opened the vault. He offered Steve Young a contract package worth more than forty million dollars!

Steve was overwhelmed. As he later told one reporter, the contract offer "was like winning the lottery." He had known he would make money in professional football, but he had never dreamed it would be that much. Money had never been important. After all, he was still driving a 1965 Oldsmobile. Still, forty million dollars was hard to ignore. Steve Young asked his father for advice.

Grit Young didn't hesitate. He told his son to take the USFL's offer. It was just too large to ignore.

On March 5, 1984, Steve Young signed the most lucrative contract in the history of professional football. The Bengals abandoned their plans to draft him. By March 6, everything in Steve Young's life had changed — but not necessarily for the best.

Overnight, Steve Young became what the press called "The Forty-Million-Dollar Man." The size of his contract made all his previous achievements seem unimportant. Before, most stories written about Steve had concentrated on what a great player he was on the field and what a great person he was off the field. Now the press portrayed him as a selfish, greedy kid.

Steve didn't understand the sudden criticism. After all, he hadn't forced the Express to offer him such a large contract; they had done so on their own, knowing it would bring much needed attention to the league. He had never played football or done anything in his life just for the money. But now everyone assumed that was all he cared about.

Steve didn't even know what to do with that much money. He didn't want a big house or a fancy car. His parents and family were already comfortable. It was strange. Before he signed the contract, he had been happy and satisfied with his life. He hadn't needed anything. Now, all of a sudden, he was rich. He still didn't need anything, but he wasn't very happy.

Steve regretted signing the contract almost immediately. He hated the way people looked at him now, and he felt bad that he had given up on his dream of playing in the NFL because of money. He felt just as he had during his freshman year at BYU, when he wanted to leave school and go home.

Once again, Steve Young turned to his father. "Dad," he said, "I think I've made a big mistake. I want to back out of the deal."

Although Grit Young knew that Steve was unhappy, he gave his son much the same advice he had offered him four years before. There were no quitters in the Young family. "You signed a contract," he told Steve. "You have to honor it."

Steve reluctantly agreed. Still, being wealthy beyond his wildest dreams made him very uncomfortable. Several years later he admitted that he carried his first check, worth several million dollars, around in his wallet for weeks. He was afraid to cash it.

A few days after signing, Steve reported to the Express. He knew it would take a while to learn their system, so in his first game in uniform in professional football, he watched from the sidelines as the Express defeated the Oakland Invaders 10–0. When the Express won 13–12 a week later, Steve watched again.

He hated it. Not playing made him feel like he wasn't earning his pay. But he knew he had to be patient. When Steve sat on the bench for the third game in a row and watched the Express lose to the Birmingham Bulls 13–7, he sensed his opportunity was coming. With a record of only 2–3, it was time for the Express to find out what they had paid for.

The New Jersey Generals were the Express's next opponent. The Generals were one of the best teams in the USFL, and New Jersey running back Herschel Walker was the biggest star in the league. The game was certain to get a lot of press coverage. Before the game Express head coach John Hadl told Steve he was his starting quarterback.

Steve was glad to play, and the publicity surrounding his appearance resulted in almost twenty thousand fans turning out, nearly twice the usual number. Steve played well, completing 19 of 29 passes for 163 yards and one touchdown. But Los Angeles lost, 26–10.

Not even Steve Young could win games on his own. Although the Express had a great deal of individual talent, they were a young team and prone to mistakes. The size of Steve Young's contract proved to be a distraction and set expectations for him and the team that neither could reach. Besides, he was still learning the offense.

The team continued to struggle. Steve was starting to play better, but after nine games, the team's record was only 3–6.

At the same time, the USFL was in trouble. Few teams in the league were drawing many fans. Some were in financial trouble. There were even rumors that Express owner William Oldenburg was running out of money. The press speculated that Steve Young might never see most of the money from his contract.

Yet just as everything appeared to be falling apart, the Express started playing better football. All of a sudden, they were one of the best teams in the league.

With Steve Young leading the way, they won seven of their last eight regular season games. The winning streak vaulted the Express into the USFL playoffs.

In the first game of the playoffs, the Express faced the Michigan Panthers, defending USFL champs. The two teams played one of the most remarkable — and longest — games in professional football history.

At the end of the fourth quarter, the score was tied 21–21. After only a few minutes of rest, both clubs headed back on the field to play sudden death overtime. Whoever scored first would win.

It took another 33 minutes and 33 seconds before Express running back Mel Gray broke loose for a 24-yard scoring run to give Los Angeles the win.

Steve completed 23 of 44 passes for 295 yards to help out.

A week later, the Express ran out of steam and lost to the Arizona Wranglers 35–23. Los Angeles's offensive line couldn't keep the Wranglers away from their quarterback. Steve was sacked seven times and completed only 7 of 23 passes. His first season in pro football was over.

Although Steve was pleased he had helped the Express turn their season around and make the play-offs, he was still uncertain about the future of the USFL and his part in it. Then, in midsummer, the Tampa Bay Buccaneers of the NFL acquired rights to sign Steve if he ever decided to leave the Express. Once again, Steve Young started dreaming about playing in the NFL.

In the off-season, Steve returned to BYU to finish his degree and to act as a broadcaster for BYU football. While Steve watched from the press box, the Cougars had their most successful season ever. The team went undefeated and ended the year ranked number one in the country.

As much as he enjoyed being back at BYU, he dreaded returning to Los Angeles for the 1985

USFL season. Even though some sportswriters were referring to the team as "the most talented and exciting young team in pro football," it was clear that the Express and the USFL were on their last legs.

Team owner William Oldenburg's financial empire had collapsed. The league took over operation of the team. In an effort to save money, most of the front office was let go. The league struggled to keep up its payments to Steve Young and prevent the team from folding.

It didn't help when the Express started the season by losing their first three games. But Steve didn't give up. He kept trying to win.

Then, in the fifth game of the season, against Arizona, Steve hurt his knee. For the first time in his pro career, he was forced out of the lineup due to injury. He missed three weeks.

Without him, the Express didn't win a game. More players got hurt. By the time Steve returned from the sidelines, he and his teammates were so demoralized that they played terrible football.

The team's few fans soon stopped coming to watch them play. In one game, at the Los Angeles Coliseum, a stadium with a capacity of more than one hundred thousand, fewer than five thousand people showed up. Steve had played before more fans in high school.

As the season limped to a conclusion, it became obvious that the USFL was in deep trouble. The team was having trouble paying its bills, and some players just plain quit. But Steve Young hung on. He was still under contract.

Things got so bad that before the final game of the season, the team's bus driver stopped the bus on its way to the game and announced, "I'm not moving until I get paid!" While some players yelled, only half-seriously, "Don't pay him — let's get off," Steve Young passed a hat to pay the driver his salary.

When the team arrived at the stadium, things were even worse. The Express had only thirteen healthy players on offense. Halfway through the game, Steve volunteered to play running back to help the team. His USFL career ended, not behind center, taking a snap and throwing the ball downfield, but as a fullback, blocking for another player.

After the game, the Express's fifteenth loss of the season, Steve expressed his frustration to a reporter. "It felt like a high school game," he said. "I was waiting for the cheerleaders to come running off the bus. It's hard to play football under these conditions. I really don't know what I'm going to do. I just know I can't do anything like this again."

The 1985 USFL season had been a nightmare, but Steve was beginning to dream again. When he closed his eyes, he saw himself playing quarterback in the NFL.

Chapter Five
1985-1987

The NFL at Last

As soon as the season ended, Steve Young asked agent Leigh Steinberg to get him out of the USFL. He wanted to play in the National Football League.

Steinberg agreed. The USFL wasn't doing Steve's career any good at all. He knew that the league could not afford to pay him the millions of dollars still due on his contract. Steinberg started negotiating for Steve's release.

But the USFL didn't want to give him away. In fact, they wanted back some of the money they had already paid him.

Steve Young had always said he didn't really care about the money. Now he had a chance to prove it. He paid the league back more than one million dollars in order to secure his release.

The deal was finally completed on September 9,

1985. The next day, Steve Young signed a five-year, six-million-dollar contract with the NFL's Tampa Bay Buccaneers. Finally he was where he wanted to be. In the NFL.

The Bucs weren't the best team in the NFL. In fact, they were just about the worst. That didn't matter to Steve. He was just happy to be there.

But once again, Steve Young found himself on the sidelines, playing backup quarterback while he learned another offense. While Tampa Bay coach Leeman Bennett considered him the Buccaneers' "quarterback of the future," quarterback Steve DeBerg was the Bucs' "quarterback of the present."

Another player might have been resentful of Steve Young, but DeBerg was different. At the beginning of his NFL career, he had served as a backup to Dallas Cowboy great Roger Staubach, Steve Young's boyhood hero. Staubach did all he could to help DeBerg. So when DeBerg finally became a starter himself, he returned the favor by doing whatever he could to help his backups. He was a team player.

DeBerg had often done his job too well. Earlier in his career, he had been the starting quarterback

Quarterbacking for the Brigham Young University Cougars

Now with the San Francisco 49ers, Steve Young looks to pass.

Steve Young and Joe Montana talk in the 49ers' locker room before a game.

C. B. Bridges

Skipping back into the pocket after the snap

Michael Zagaris

Here, Young has plenty of time to throw a pinpoint accurate pass, thanks to good protection from his teammates.

Michael Zagaris

Always alert, Steve Young runs the ball to gain crucial yards.

Steve Young in discussion with teammates, receivers John Taylor (82) and Jerry Rice (80)

His uniform muddy from a day's hard work, Steve Young fades back for a pass.

Steve Young lets a pass fly moments before being tackled.

Steve Young's elation after winning Super Bowl XXIX is obvious.

Steve Young's Year-to-Year Statistics

Year/Team	Attempts	Completions	Percentage	Yards	Touchdowns	Interceptions
1980—1981 BYU	112	56	.500	731	5	Not Available
1981—1982 BYU	367	230	.627	3100	18	Not Available
1982—1983 BYU	429	306	.713	3902	33	Not Available
College Totals	908	592	.652	7733	56	Not Available
1983—1984 Express	310	179	.577	2361	10	9
1984—1985 Express	250	137	.548	1741	6	13
1985—1986 Buccaneers	138	72	.522	935	3	8
1986—1987 Buccaneers	363	195	.537	2282	8	3
1986—1987 49ers	69	37	.536	570	10	0
1987—1988 49ers	101	54	.535	680	3	3
1988—1989 49ers	92	64	.696	1001	8	3
1989—1990 49ers	62	38	.613	427	2	0
1990—1991 49ers	279	180	.645	2517	17	8
1991—1992 49ers	402	268	.667	3465	25	7
1992—1993 49ers	462	314	.680	4023	29	16
1993—1994 49ers	461	324	.703	3969	35	10
Pro Totals 12 Years	2989	1862	.623	23971	156	90

Steve Young's Career Highlights

1983: NCAA Leader in Total Offense:
359.1 yards per game (a national record)
Consensus All-American
Heisman Trophy Runnerup
Davey O'Brien Award

1984: Passed for 300 yards in two games
Rushed for 100 yards in one game

1985: Rushed for 100 yards in one game

1990: Rushed for 100 yards in one game

1991: Passed for 300 yards in three games

1992: Passed for 300 yards in three games
NFL Player of the Year (*The Sporting News*)
NFL All-Pro Quarterback (*The Sporting News*)
Pro Bowl

1993: Passed for 300 yards in three games
Pro Bowl

1994: Passed for 300 yards in five games
NFL Player of the Year (*The Sporting News*)
NFL All-Pro Quarterback (*The Sporting News*)
Pro Bowl
MVP of Super Bowl XXIX

Holds NFL career records for:

- highest completion percentage (.636)
- highest passer rating (96.8)
- most consecutive seasons leading league in passer rating
  (4 total, 1991–1994)

Holds NFL single season record for highest passer rating (1994)

for the San Francisco 49ers. When the 49ers drafted Notre Dame quarterback Joe Montana, DeBerg took Montana under his wing, only to watch Montana take his job. After DeBerg was traded to the Denver Broncos, the same thing happened as Denver drafted backup quarterback John Elway. Still, despite this pattern, DeBerg reached out his hand to help Steve Young.

Each week, Steve practiced with the team and learned a little bit more about the Bucs' offense and life in the NFL. Then each Sunday he stood on the sidelines and watched as the Bucs took a beating on the field. Although he tried to be patient, he desperately wanted to play.

In the twelfth game of the season, the New York Jets, hardly the best team in the league, destroyed the Bucs 62–28. All game long, Tampa Bay fans chanted, "We want Young! We want Young!" After the game, Coach Bennett announced that Steve Young was now his starting quarterback.

At last! Steve Young's dream was going to come true. He practiced hard all week, and when he ran onto the field as the Bucs played host to the Detroit Lions, he could hardly contain his excitement.

It didn't take long for the Lions to settle him down. The Bucs' offensive line was almost helpless against the Lions' pass rush, and Steve spent much of the game racing around the field trying to avoid being sacked. Entering the third quarter, the Bucs trailed 13–6. Young had passed for only 38 yards.

Detroit added a field goal to increase their lead to 16–6. Then, with just under four minutes left in the game, Buc running back James Wilder bulled across the goal line to make the score 16–13. The Bucs got the ball back a few minutes later.

All of a sudden, Steve found his passing rhythm. He quickly led the Bucs downfield. They tied the game with a field goal and sent the game into over-time.

Once again, Steve led the Bucs into field goal range. When the kick split the uprights, the Bucs won, 19–16, only their second victory of the season. But with Steve Young at quarterback, the Bucs were 1–0.

That was the highlight of the season. Tampa Bay went on to drop the next two games, finishing at 2–14. In the off-season, Steve worked out more than ever before. He wanted to make sure he was ready for the 1986 season. Now that he was the starting quarterback, he was determined to try to lead the Bucs into the playoffs.

Steve Young began the exhibition season as the number one quarterback, but after only a few weeks, Coach Bennett announced that he had decided to go with DeBerg again. He didn't think Steve Young understood the Buc offense, and he disliked the fact that when Steve felt too much pressure from the defense, he took off and ran with the ball. Unlike most quarterbacks, Steve never ducked out of bounds or slid to the ground to avoid being hit. He put his head down and ran like a halfback.

The Bucs opened their season playing host to the San Francisco 49ers. San Francisco quarterback Joe Montana had a day like one Steve Young had had once for BYU. Montana shredded the Buc defense for 346 passing yards. Steve DeBerg, on the other hand, threw seven interceptions. The 49ers won in a rout.

Steve Young couldn't understand why he wasn't put in the game. Tampa Bay lost again the following week as he watched helplessly from the bench.

Finally Coach Bennett decided he had seen

enough of DeBerg. He announced that Steve Young would start for the Bucs in their next game, against Detroit.

The weeks on the sidelines had taken their toll. Steve had a terrible game. He threw for only 39 yards. But somehow the Bucs won. That was enough to earn him another start.

Steve hoped to lead the team on a winning streak and into the playoffs. After all, it was still early in the season.

Each of the next two games, against Atlanta and Los Angeles, went into overtime. Each time, the Bucs lost.

The narrow defeats demoralized the team. The Tampa Bay players were used to losing, but after coming so close to winning and falling short, they started giving up.

Each week, the Bucs played worse than the week before. Although Steve sometimes played well, nothing he did seemed to make a difference. The remainder of the season was a rerun of the experience Young had had with Los Angeles in his second season in the USFL. The injuries piled up, and Steve started taking a beating.

In the last home game of the season, against Green Bay, disgusted Tampa Bay fans threw lemons on the field and booed and jeered all game long as the Bucs lost 21–7. A week later, Tampa lost to St. Louis as the season mercifully came to an end. The Bucs finished a disastrous 2–14, the worst record in the entire league. The only thing Steve Young's Bucs won was the right to make the first pick in the 1987 NFL draft. Soon after the season ended, Tampa Bay announced that they intended to use that draft pick to select a quarterback.

As far as the Bucs were concerned, "the quarterback of the future" had become "the quarterback of the past." Steve Young was history. Although he was bitterly disappointed, Steve didn't blame them. After all, in nineteen games as Tampa Bay's starting quarterback over two seasons, he had led the Bucs to only three wins. But he also knew he hadn't had much help. When the Bucs drafted University of Miami quarterback Vinnie Testaverde with their first pick, Steve figured his days in Tampa Bay were numbered. The Bucs weren't going to pay him a million dollars a year just to sit on the bench.

Everything was falling apart. After four years in

pro football, Young was viewed by many people as a failure. Statistically he was one of the worst quarterbacks in the league. Jim McMahon, whom Steve had succeeded at BYU, had become a star with the Chicago Bears and led the team to a Super Bowl win in 1986. Steve Young was still considered just another good college quarterback. Some people were beginning to consider him a has-been at age twenty-five.

He tried to go on with his life. In the off-season, he bought a big house back in Utah and planned to get married. He looked forward to starting a family and settling down. But the night before the wedding, after all his friends had flown into Provo, he called the wedding off.

He didn't bother to move into his new home. Instead, he moved into an old pioneer house no bigger than a studio apartment. He tried to concentrate on law school, played around on his piano, and thought about the future. He had never given up before, but for the first time in his life, Steve Young began to wonder if he would ever fulfill his dreams. Despite all his hard work and patience, four years after leaving college he was uncertain of what the future held.

Generations before, his great-great-great-grandfather had faced a similar situation. When Brigham Young first came to Utah, the future looked very bleak indeed. Yet he had persevered. Now it was time for Steve Young to take a lesson from his famous ancestor. This was no time to give up.

Chapter Six
1987–1990

Backup Again

Lucky for Steve Young, there were still a few people in the NFL who looked beyond Tampa Bay's won-lost record and Young's own statistics to see a talented player full of potential. Despite the fact that Steve expected the Bucs to try and trade him, in the spring of 1987 he attended Tampa Bay's minicamp. At camp, Steve DeBerg told him that to be successful, he just needed a chance to learn the professional game from some talented coaches. DeBerg suggested that he try to get himself traded to the San Francisco 49ers.

San Francisco coach Bill Walsh was considered by many to be a coaching genius. Walsh loved the pass and had developed a complex, highly effective offense based on the passing game. The 49ers sometimes passed the ball forty or fifty times a game. They were one of the most successful teams in the NFL and had won the Super Bowl in both 1982 and 1984. And now Bill Walsh was interested in Steve Young.

Walsh had been a Steve Young fan since Young had starred for BYU. Walsh and BYU coach LaVell Edwards were good friends, and Edwards had always spoken highly of Steve, not just for his physical talent, but for his intelligence, character, and leadership ability as well. To run the 49er offense, a quarterback needed precisely those qualities. Furthermore, Walsh's quarterback coach, Mike Holmgren, had been one of Steve's coaches at BYU. He, too, was a Steve Young fan.

There was just one problem. The 49ers already had a quarterback. Joe Montana. And Joe Montana was not just any quarterback. He was the best quarterback in pro football.

Montana was perfect for Walsh's system, which emphasized short passes that allowed San Francisco to control the ball for long periods of the game. Montana's arm wasn't particularly strong, but he was smart, mobile, and made great decisions on the field. There was no better quarterback in the league late in the game.

But if Montana had a flaw, it was his health. In 1986, Montana had injured his back and missed much of the season. During the playoffs, he had been hurt again. Walsh was dissatisfied with his backup quarterbacks and wanted to make sure that if Montana went down again, the 49ers had a signal caller who could run their complicated offense. He wanted Steve Young to be that player.

Word of Walsh's interest soon reached Steve's ears. The more he thought about wearing the scarlet-and-gold 49er uniform, the better he liked the idea. Although he didn't relish the idea of playing second string, he believed that the opportunity to learn from Bill Walsh offset playing second fiddle to Montana. He was also confident in his own ability. He liked the challenge that playing behind Montana would present. He thought he could eventually win the starting job on his own. Besides, the 49ers were one of the best teams in the league. After four dismal seasons, Young was tired of playing for the worst teams.

Soon after the Bucs signed Testaverde to a contract, Steve Young told agent Leigh Steinberg to ask the Bucs to trade him. If at all possible, Steve wanted to go to San Francisco.

The Bucs agreed to look into a trade, but like the USFL a few seasons before, Tampa Bay had no intention of giving him away. They announced that the price for Steve Young would be a first-round and a third-round draft pick.

The high asking price scared off every team interested in him, even the 49ers. But by this time, the Bucs were committed to a trade. They soon lowered their demands to a second- and a fourth-round pick.

That was fine with the 49ers. On April 24, 1987, Steve Young became a member of the San Francisco 49ers.

Steve spent much of the summer getting in shape and trying to figure out the 49ers' complicated playbook. When training camp began, he went about the task of playing behind Joe Montana.

Montana wasn't worried about Steve Young. He was the best quarterback on the best team in pro football, and he knew it. While he wasn't mean to Steve Young, he wasn't exactly Steve DeBerg, either. Montana's biggest concern was getting himself ready for the season. He didn't consider helping Steve Young to be part of his job.

But just as Walsh had worried, Joe Montana was injured during the exhibition season. Although Montana missed only one game, Steve Young finally had a chance to demonstrate what he could do in the NFL.

Steve started the 49ers' final exhibition game against the Los Angeles Raiders. He showed San Francisco fans that he was a much different quarterback from Joe Montana.

Whereas Montana was methodical and precise, Steve Young was dashing and daring. When Montana was forced to scramble, he usually either threw the ball away, dashed out of bounds, or slid to his knees to avoid getting hurt. But when Steve Young had to scramble, look out!

In the game against the Raiders, Steve played as if he'd never have a chance to play again. When he had the time, he threw quickly and accurately. When he didn't, he showed that he was one of the most exciting runners in the league. San Francisco fans weren't used to seeing a quarterback put his head down and run over tacklers. All by himself, Steve was responsible for more offensive yardage than the entire Raiders team. San Francisco won easily.

Young hoped his performance would impress Walsh enough to name him starting quarterback. But when the season opened a week later, Joe Montana took the field to start the game. Steve Young was on the sidelines again.

It didn't take long for him to get frustrated. Only a few weeks into the season, he began to regret his decision to come to San Francisco. Soon, he was on the phone to his father again.

Grit Young still gave Steve the same advice he always had. No one in the Young family was a quitter. Patience had taken Steve Young a long way from the junior varsity at Greenwich High. There was no reason to believe it wouldn't take him further.

For most of the season, Steve hardly played. When he did, the 49ers were way ahead in the game. Still, he played well whenever he had the chance. Meanwhile, he learned all that he could by watching Joe Montana and listening to his coaches.

Late in the season, the 49ers faced the Chicago Bears on a Monday night at San Francisco's Candlestick Park. Both teams were 10–2, tied for the best record in the league. Football fans all over the nation tuned in to watch on *Monday Night Football*.

Bear quarterback Jim McMahon, Young's old teammate at BYU, would miss the game with a pulled hamstring. Facing a McMahon-less Chicago, Joe Montana and the 49ers were expected to win big.

Early in the first quarter, Joe Montana dropped back to pass. The Bears forced him out of the pocket, and Montana sprinted out of bounds to avoid being sacked. Just as he reached the safety of the sidelines, he grabbed the back of his thigh and fell down.

The crowd in Candlestick Park watched breathlessly as Montana gingerly stood up and limped off the field. Like McMahon, he, too, had pulled a hamstring muscle. Montana was out of the game.

Steve Young saw Montana go down and started warming up. Without waiting to be told, he ran onto the field and took over.

The 49ers' fans were anxious. Except for the game against the Raiders in the exhibition season, they hadn't seen that much of their new backup quarterback. With the playoffs approaching, and Montana hurt, they wondered if Steve Young could handle the 49er offense.

In the huddle, Steve looked around at his teammates. He was nervous, but he didn't dare let his teammates know. They looked to him to lead the way.

He thought for a moment and called out the play. His teammates paused, then enthusiastically broke from the huddle. For his first play, Steve Young called something that Joe Montana would never have called in a million years: a "keeper." He would carry the ball himself.

The 49ers lined up, and Steve called out the signals as the powerful Bear defense dug in. They had already knocked Montana out of the game. Now they wanted Steve Young.

Steve took the snap and rolled to his left. Then he cut upfield behind a block and broke into the Chicago secondary. He danced outside and left a Bear linebacker clawing at the air. Then he sprinted down the sideline.

Chicago's cornerback came up to make the tackle. He had the angle on Steve and expected the quarterback to head out of bounds. The cornerback reached out to give him a shove.

Pow! Steve Young put down his shoulder and

plowed into the cornerback's midsection. The Bear defender flew backwards! Steve ran right over him before several Bears finally piled on his back and brought him down.

"First down, San Francisco!" screamed the stadium's announcer. "An 18-yard gain for quarterback Steve Young." The fans roared their approval. Back in the San Francisco huddle, Steve Young looked confidently at his teammates. He had waited a long time for this.

The keeper confused the Bear defense and kept them off balance the rest of the game. They weren't sure if Steve Young was going to pass the ball or run. They guessed wrong all night.

Steve destroyed the Bears' defense, throwing four touchdown passes. The 49ers beat Chicago 41–0. It was a big win. The 49ers all but clinched home field advantage in the post-season, and Steve Young had proven he could run the 49er offense.

But Montana healed quickly, and within a week Steve was back on the bench. When the playoffs started a few weeks later, the 49ers were favored to reach the Super Bowl with Montana at the helm.

San Francisco faced the Minnesota Vikings in the

first round of the playoffs at Candlestick Park. For most of the game, the 49ers were terrible while the Vikings were terrific.

In the first half, Minnesota plowed through the 49ers at will on their way to 20 first-half points. On defense, the Vikings hounded Joe Montana into one of the worst performances of his career. The field was wet and sloppy, and Montana couldn't seem to get comfortable. His only touchdown pass was an interception run back for a score by Minnesota.

After halftime, things got worse. Early in the third quarter, with Minnesota leading 27–10, the 49ers were forced to punt. As Joe Montana stepped off the field and pulled loose the chin strap on his helmet, Bill Walsh put his hand on his shoulder.

"Joe," he snapped, "I'm going with Steve." Montana was benched for the first time in his career!

Minnesota punted, and the 49ers took over. Steve Young came in at quarterback.

For the rest of the game, 49er fans witnessed the "Steve Young Show." Just as he had done against the Bears a few weeks before, he combined the run and the pass to befuddle the Minnesota defense.

But it was too little, too late. Despite passing for 158 yards and running for 72 more, Young ran out of time and the Vikings won. San Francisco's season was over.

For the first time in a long time, Steve Young couldn't wait for the next season to begin. In limited duty in 1987, he had completed 37 of 69 passes. Ten of those had gone for touchdowns. In 1988, Steve hoped to play his way into the 49er starting lineup.

In the exhibition season, he split time with Joe Montana. Then, just before the season began, Coach Walsh told a sportswriter that his only worry during the upcoming season was that "We might have a quarterback controversy."

Steve took that to mean that he had a chance to beat out Joe Montana for the starting job. Montana took that to mean that Walsh was giving up on him.

All of a sudden Walsh was in an uncomfortable position. No matter how hard he tried, there was no way to keep both quarterbacks happy.

In preseason play, Steve Young clearly outplayed Joe Montana. At the same time, there were rumors that the 49ers were entertaining trade offers for

Montana. It looked as if Steve Young had the inside track to the starting job.

But just before the season started, Walsh named Montana his starting quarterback. It was back to the sidelines for Steve Young. He was crushed.

Then Walsh surprised everyone. Although Montana would start the 49ers' first game, Walsh announced that Steve Young would start the second game.

It was a curious strategy, one that made neither quarterback very happy. Montana won the first game, and when Young stumbled in week two, Montana came off the bench to lead the 49ers on a come-from-behind win. His performance appeared to earn him the starting spot.

But Montana just couldn't stay healthy. His back was giving him fits. Although he was clearly the number one quarterback, whenever Montana was injured or needed a rest, Walsh didn't hesitate to bring in Steve Young.

To each quarterback's credit, they never allowed the controversy to affect the team's performance. The current situation was something neither player could control. Although they hardly talked to each other, each knew the other was playing as well as he possibly could.

In fact, it really didn't matter who took the snaps from the center. The 49ers were the best team in the league, and whoever was playing quarterback was usually the best quarterback in the league. Late in the season, as Montana stepped out of the lineup with back spasms, Steve Young got another start.

The 49ers' opponent was Minnesota, the same team that had bumped them from the playoffs in 1987. Once again, the Vikings vaulted to an early lead.

Although he played poorly in the first half, Steve got hot after halftime and led the 49ers to two scores. But with just over two minutes to play, the Vikings led, 21–17.

San Francisco had the ball on the Minnesota 49. A player ran in from the bench with the next play, a pass over the middle. The 49ers broke from the huddle, and Steve Young crouched behind the center.

As he called out the signals, Steve glanced at the Viking defense. The play called for him to throw the ball to wide receiver Mike Wilson in the middle of the field. Steve wanted to make sure he knew where every player in the Minnesota secondary was lined up.

The center snapped the ball, and Steve retreated in the pocket. He tried to look downfield, but all he saw were the purple-and-white jerseys of Minnesota's huge defensive line. His pass protection had broken down!

Steve didn't panic, but he also didn't hesitate. He saw a small gap open up between rushers, so he tucked the ball beneath his arm and started running.

As soon as he broke free of the line, Steve saw Minnesota safety Joey Browner closing fast. Browner reached out for him, but Steve angled away and Browner couldn't hold on.

That gave Viking lineman Keith Millard a chance to catch up. He came at Steve from the side. But the quarterback cut the opposite direction, and Millard ended up with an armful of air.

Steve picked his way upfield, legs churning. With each step, it seemed as if another Minnesota Viking got a piece of him, but he stutter-stepped, cut back, spun, bounced, or danced out of the way. Somehow he stayed on his feet.

As Steve bounced off tacklers, he kept going forward, toward the goal line. With each miss, the Candlestick Park crowd roared a little louder. By the time the quarterback reached the ten-yard line, everyone was on their feet cheering!

Steve Young was like the milk bottle in a carnival game. No matter how hard he was hit, he refused to fall. Just inside the ten-yard line, one last tackler banged into him from the side, but he still refused to go down. Off balance, he lurched toward the end zone. Stumbling and straining to stay on his feet, he caught sight of the goal line and dove headlong, stretching the ball out ahead of him.

As he hit the turf, the ball edged across the line. The referee threw his hands into the air. Touchdown!

Steve Young lay on the ground, exhausted, as the hoarse cheers of sixty-nine thousand fans swirled through the air around him. Then he was surrounded by red-and-gold jerseys. His teammates lifted him to his feet and half-carried him back to the 49er bench.

Eight different Vikings had had a chance to tackle him. Steve Young had made all eight miss.

The 49ers won. Young's performance earned him the NFL's Player of the Week award. But long after the week was over, no one could stop talking about Steve Young's unbelievable run.

In the history of the National Football League, there have been some amazing players and some amazing runs. Running backs like Jim Brown, Gale Sayers, Walter Payton, Barry Sanders, and Emmitt Smith have thrilled fans with their incredible ability.

In 1994, as part of the NFL's seventy-fifth anniversary celebration, the league polled sportswriters to select the best run in the entire history of the National Football League. The writers didn't select a run by Brown, Sayers, Sanders, or any of the hundreds of men who have earned a living in the National Football League for their ability to run with the ball. They selected Steve Young's mad scramble as the best run ever in the NFL.

But even that historic run wasn't enough to make Steve Young the 49ers' number one quarterback. Montana took over as soon as his back was healed.

It would be hard to argue with Coach Walsh's decision. With Montana at the helm of the 49er offense, San Francisco surged into the playoffs and won the NFC championship and the right to play the Cincinnati Bengals in Super Bowl XXIII.

For Steve Young, the Super Bowl experience was eerily familiar. Just as he had stood on the sidelines and watched Jim McMahon lead the BYU Cougars in the Holiday Bowl, now he watched Montana lead the 49ers. Although San Francisco struggled for much of the game, Bill Walsh never put Steve Young onto the field.

With only three minutes and ten seconds left to play, San Francisco took possession. They were trailing 16–13 and were 92 yards away from the end zone.

Joe Montana responded with just about the best three minutes of football he had ever played in his life. Calmly and methodically, Montana moved the 49ers down the field. With thirty seconds left, he hit wide receiver John Taylor in the middle of the end zone for the winning score. The San Francisco 49ers were Super Bowl champions for the third time in Joe Montana's career.

Known simply as "The Drive," Montana's performance in the last minutes of Super Bowl XXIII solidified his grip on the quarterback position. In the off-season, while Steve Young returned to Utah and began attending law school part-time, coach Bill Walsh retired. The first thing new coach George Seifert did was announce that there was no quarterback controversy. Joe Montana was his number one quarterback.

For the next two seasons, Steve Young sat on the bench as Joe Montana led the best team in the National Football League. In 1989, Young started three regular season games when Montana was hurt, but he saw only mop-up duty in Super Bowl XXIV. The Montana-led 49ers destroyed the Denver Broncos 55–10 to win their second straight world championship.

The 1990 season continued to try Young's patience. He paced on the sidelines while Montana starred. He played less than he had in any season since his freshman year at BYU, appearing in only six regular season games, including only one start, and throwing only 62 passes.

Once the playoffs began, it was more of the same. Steve Young didn't play in the opening round. But in the NFC championship game against the New York Giants, Montana struggled.

In the game's final minutes, Montana was sacked and broke a finger on his throwing hand. Young entered the game with the 49ers behind 15–13. If he could lead them to victory, he would start Super Bowl XXV, because Montana would be unable to play. This was Steve Young's big chance.

He had the 49ers driving when the season ended on a fumble by 49er running back Roger Craig. The Giants took over and were able to run out the clock. There would be no Super Bowl for Steve Young in 1990.

Steve had tried to remain patient, but he was still just a second-string quarterback. Although everyone said he was the best second-string quarterback in the NFL, that didn't make him feel much better. As he sat in his law school classes a few weeks after the Super Bowl, he found it hard to concentrate.

As difficult as the past season had been, Steve Young still kept dreaming about starting as quarterback.

Chapter Seven
1990-1993

A Tale of Two Quarterbacks

In the off-season, Steve Young was a changed man.

His patience was just about gone. After waiting for his chance to start for the 49ers for four seasons, he seemed no closer than when he had first joined the team, in 1987. His contract was up, and he told a reporter that he felt "very overqualified" to play second-string quarterback. So Young told Leigh Steinberg to approach the 49ers and ask about a trade. He didn't want to play behind Joe Montana anymore. Privately he referred to Montana as "the quarterback who wouldn't die," a grudging compliment to Montana for his uncanny ability to bounce back from injuries. If Steve Young couldn't play in San Francisco, he knew there must be some team in the NFL that wanted him.

There were. Almost every team in the league

wanted him. But when Steinberg asked the 49ers about a trade, they made it clear that in any trade involving Steve Young, San Francisco wanted draft picks rather than veteran players. The only teams that would be able to trade for him would be those that had won only a handful of games the year before.

For Steve Young, such a trade would be like returning to Tampa Bay. He told a reporter that he would "rather go be a lawyer" than play for a team that had no chance of winning. So in May 1991, he signed another contract to stay in San Francisco.

He was soon glad he did. In the preseason, Montana was bothered by elbow trouble in his throwing arm. When the elbow was examined, doctors discovered a torn tendon. If Montana ever wanted to play again, he would have to have the tendon replaced. Rehabilitation from that kind of surgery took more than a year.

All of a sudden, Steve Young was the 49ers' starting quarterback. Montana had the surgery and would miss at least the rest of the season. By that time, Steve Young wanted to make sure there would be no question about who was the number one quarterback. At long last, his patience was paying off.

He began the 1991 season as if he were trying to make up for lost time. In the 49ers' first game, against the New York Giants, he threw for a 78-yard touchdown pass and ran for another score. A week later, against San Diego, he completed 26 passes for 348 yards.

The 49ers were scoring points like no other team in the league. Not even Joe Montana's 49ers had ever been this potent. Not that Steve Young didn't have help. His supporting cast was the best in the league.

In some people's minds, San Francisco wide receiver Jerry Rice, was, and still is, the best receiver of all time. Despite usually being covered by two men, Rice is the most dangerous receiver in the league.

The 49ers' other wide receiver, John Taylor, was nearly as good as Rice. If the defense ignored him, Taylor usually made them pay. With Rice and Taylor on the receiving end of his passes, Steve Young's job was made easier.

And if the opposition somehow stopped the 49er passing game, they still had to contend with Steve's own running ability and that of running back Roger

Craig. Each could break loose for a big gain at any time, making it impossible for a defense to focus entirely on the pass.

As the 1991 season progressed, Steve Young kept getting better and better. After passing for 348 yards and running for two touchdowns against Atlanta in early October, he set a 49er record when he completed 18 of 20 passes for two touchdowns a week later. For the month, he made nearly 70 percent of his passes and was named NFC Offensive Player of the Month.

But some people still kept comparing him to Joe Montana. No matter what he did, in some people's eyes he would never measure up to the fallen 49er quarterback. Montana specialized in fourth-quarter comebacks, something Steve Young had yet to do. Each time he made a mistake, no matter how small, some 49er fans turned to one another and said, "Joe wouldn't have done that."

Steve tried to ignore the criticism. He knew he couldn't win in a war of words against a legend. He had to play the game on the field.

But the 49ers were in transition. Despite Steve's

own stellar performance, San Francisco was playing only .500 football. Everyone looked to Steve Young to get the team going.

In a rematch against Atlanta, on November 3, it seemed as if he was ready to do just that. Early in the game, the 49ers had the ball on their own three-yard line.

In similar situations, most teams try to run the ball before trying a pass. And even if they do pass, they usually play it safe. An interception on a pass thrown from the three-yard line can easily be turned into a touchdown.

But Steve Young wasn't one to play it safe. He knew the Falcons would stack the line to try to prevent the run. He also knew that they would still assign two players to cover Jerry Rice, just in case. That meant that John Taylor would be covered by only one man. If Taylor got behind the defense, he could go all the way.

Young called a play that sent Rice to one side of the field and Taylor to the other. He took the snap, dropped back, and looked in Rice's direction.

Sure enough, two defenders were running stride-for-stride with Rice. Young lifted his arm and faked a pass Rice's way.

Then he looked toward Taylor. The fake had worked! The defender covering Taylor had hesitated when Young faked, giving Taylor a chance to sneak past him.

Steve lofted the ball deep downfield. The defender turned and scrambled after Taylor.

He may as well have tried to catch a speeding train. Taylor was three steps behind him and pulling away. He caught the ball in full stride and raced to the end zone for a 97-yard touchdown reception. Six points for San Francisco!

Steve Young was at the top of his game. When San Francisco got the ball back a few minutes later, he led them down the field once again.

Then catastrophe struck. After letting a pass go, a rushing Atlanta defensive lineman slipped and rolled into Steve Young's knee. Steve dropped to the ground, wincing in pain.

He limped off the field a few minutes later. He had torn a ligament in his knee.

Although the injury hurt, doctors told him he would be able to return to action in three or four weeks. Steve was relieved. He didn't want anything to keep him from the Super Bowl.

But as Steve stood on the sidelines the next several weeks, he watched his backup, former UCLA quarterback Steve Bono, step in and do a fair imitation of Joe Montana. Bono played so well that some fans and sportswriters suggested that the 49ers make him the permanent starter.

That was just what Steve Young needed! To finally get his chance to step from Montana's shadow only to have his backup take over!

The 49er coaches kept silent on the subject. In December, Steve was well enough to be in uniform but didn't play in either of the next two games. The coaches told the press that they were just waiting for his knee to fully heal.

Oddly, Steve didn't complain. He later told a reporter that while watching Bono run the 49er offense, he had realized that "it was my job to orchestrate the offense, not play every instrument. . . . I knew I had to relax more and let everything come together. I discovered I just had to be me and play ball." Besides, the 49ers were 5–1 with Steve Bono at quarterback.

On December 14, the 49ers played the Kansas

City Chiefs. In the third quarter, Bono went down hard and got up limping. He had hurt his knee. Steve Young was back in the lineup.

He picked up right where he had left off. In the final regular season game of the year, against the mighty Chicago Bears, Steve Young was magnificent. He completed 21 of 32 passes for 338 yards and three touchdowns. When no one was open, he proved that his knee was healthy by dashing for 63 yards and a touchdown himself. The 49ers won 52–14.

But it wasn't enough. San Francisco finished the season with a disappointing 10–6 record. Although Steve Young led the NFL in quarterback ratings, the 49ers didn't even qualify for the playoffs. In the off-season, 49er fans started talking about Joe Montana again.

At first it looked as if Montana was ready to take his old job back. When the team held minicamp in the spring of 1992, 49er coaches were thrilled to see that Montana was throwing the ball better than ever before.

The 49ers didn't want a quarterback controversy. They realized that the situation made neither Young nor Montana happy, not to mention Steve Bono, who rightly thought his 1991 performance earned him a chance to play. For a while, they tried to trade Steve Young.

Fortunately no one offered San Francisco enough to make a trade. When Montana reinjured his elbow in preseason, Steve Young's spot on the 49ers was secure again, at least for a while.

The 49ers improved in 1992, and so did Steve Young — although he did receive a scare in the opening game of the season against the New York Giants, when he was knocked out of the game with a concussion. He recovered, and the next week against Buffalo threw for a career-high 449 yards and three touchdowns. The 49ers were on their way.

While the team stormed through the regular season, Joe Montana finally healed and started campaigning for playing time. He was still wildly popular with San Francisco fans, and many thought the 49ers had a better chance to go to the Super Bowl with Montana at quarterback.

In the final game of the season, on a Monday night against the Detroit Lions, the 49ers decided to see if Montana was ready. Privately, San Francisco's coaching staff was discussing trading Montana and wanted to give other teams in the NFL a chance to take a look at him. They announced that Steve Young would play the first half of the game but Joe Montana would play the second half.

Steve played well, completing 12 of 18 passes, a performance good enough to secure his second straight NFL passing title. But in the second half, all eyes were on Montana.

He turned in a vintage performance. Despite not having played in almost two seasons, Montana shredded the Detroit secondary with a series of pin-point passes and drove the 49ers to 17 quick points and a win.

After the game, all 49er fans could talk about was Joe Montana. They forgot all about how well Steve Young had played in the first half and ignored the fact that the game meant nothing to either team. Detroit, who finished the season with a record of only 5–11, hadn't even used many of its starting players in the second half against Montana.

Despite pressure from the fans, when the playoffs started, Steve Young was still at quarterback for the 49ers. He had played too well and for too long for the 49ers to bench him. For the second year in a row, he finished with the highest quarterback rating in the league, and he also led the NFL with 26 touchdown passes and a completion percentage of 66.7. The 49ers finished 14–2 and won the Western Division championship. Steve Young was named the NFL's Most Valuable Player. The Super Bowl was the only challenge that still remained for Steve Young's 49ers.

But before they reached the Super Bowl, the 49ers had to go through the Dallas Cowboys. And the Cowboys would prove to be Steve Young's greatest challenge yet.

The Cowboys reminded many people of the 49ers a decade before, when Joe Montana had led them to the first of his four Super Bowl wins. The Cowboys were younger and faster than San Francisco and were led by a young quarterback, Troy Aikman, whom some observers were calling the best quarterback in pro football since Montana. The Cowboys were at least as talented as San Francisco and lacked only the 49ers' experience.

They picked up all the experience they needed in the 1992 NFC championship game.

At first it looked as if the 49ers would win big. On

the third play of the game, Steve faded back and spotted some blitzing Cowboy linebackers. He immediately knew that this meant wide receiver Jerry Rice was covered by only one defender. And no one man could cover Jerry Rice.

Without even looking in Rice's direction, Steve rifled a pass to where he knew the wide receiver would be. As soon as the ball left his hand, he was knocked to the ground.

He had guessed right. Rice was open, took the pass in full stride, and loped into the end zone for a touchdown. At least that's what Rice thought.

He hadn't heard the referee's whistle or seen the yellow penalty marker flying through the air. One of the 49ers' offensive linemen was caught holding. The play was called back.

The 49ers were forced to punt. A few plays later, Dallas went ahead 3–0 on a field goal.

But the 49ers returned the kickoff for 50 yards, and Steve Young marched the team in for a touchdown, crossing the goal line himself on a one-yard plunge. At the end of the first quarter, San Francisco led 7–3.

The two teams traded points for the next two

quarters, and at the beginning of the final period Dallas led 17–13.

San Francisco fans had always looked forward to situations like this. This was when Joe Montana always rallied his team from behind. They wondered if Steve Young could do the same.

They were disappointed. Twice Steve misread the Cowboys' pass coverage and threw two critical interceptions. The Cowboys controlled the ball behind the running of Emmitt Smith and pushed across two touchdowns. When Young finally drove the 49ers down the field for another score, he did so amid chants of "We want Joe! We want Joe!" In the fans' eyes and on the scoreboard, the touchdown was too little, too late. The Cowboys won 30–20. Once again, there would be no Super Bowl for Steve Young and the 49ers.

After the game, Young felt as bad as he had ever felt after any football game in his life. In a press conference, he told reporters, "It's tough to put into words, but you can imagine that around here we really expect to go all the way each year. I'm not sure what to say at this point. It hurts."

While Steve patiently continued to answer all the

reporters' questions, Joe Montana left the club-house without talking to anyone. On a San Francisco sports talk radio show after the game, caller after caller suggested that the 49ers trade one of their two quarterbacks: Steve Young. "Young," said one caller, "has got to go. We want Joe." Most 49er fans seemed to agree.

In the off-season, the 49er front office weighed its options. They were paying the salaries of two start-ing quarterbacks but needed only one. They had to choose between Joe Montana and Steve Young.

It made more sense to keep Steve. He was younger than Montana, healthy, and had just com-pleted two of the greatest seasons an NFL quarter-back ever had. Montana was older, injury prone, and had hardly played in two years.

But Montana was much more popular with the fans. And besides, he had proven he could take the team to the Super Bowl and win. In fact, he had done so four times. Steve Young hadn't even won an NFC championship.

By early April, the 49ers knew they had to make their move.

At first the 49ers decided to keep Joe Montana

and trade Steve Young for a top draft pick, which they planned to use to select a rookie quarterback they could groom as Montana's replacement. But no one would give the 49ers the high draft pick they wanted.

So San Francisco changed gears. Now, they decided, they would keep *Young* and trade *Montana.* They even gave Montana the right to decide where he would be traded and make his own deal. In a few days, he came back to the 49ers and announced he had worked out a trade to the Kansas City Chiefs.

Then the 49ers waffled. All of a sudden, they didn't want to trade Montana anymore. They told him that if he stayed, they'd make him the starting quarterback. Steve Young, the best passer in the NFL over the past two seasons, would be the backup again.

Everyone expected Young to explode at the news. But he remained quiet. He had been through so much, he knew better than to get into a public argument with the 49ers. He decided to remain silent and see what happened next. He could afford to be patient.

The 49ers expected Montana to leap at their offer. But Montana turned them down.

He announced that he was offended by the way
the 49ers kept changing their minds and felt he now
had a commitment to play in Kansas City. Besides,
Montana didn't want to look over his shoulder and
see Steve Young. Steve wasn't the new kid on the
block anymore but an experienced veteran.
Montana knew it would be hard to keep his job.

On April 16, the 49ers agreed to the trade. Joe
Montana became a member of the Kansas City
Chiefs, and Steve Young was, finally, at last and
without question, the 49ers' quarterback.

All he had to do to make everyone happy was win
the Super Bowl.

That wasn't going to be easy. Although Young set
more records in 1993, won the NFL passing title
for the third consecutive year, and beat numerous
49er team records held by Joe Montana, he failed
in the one area where everyone still compared him
to the 49ers' former quarterback. For the second
year in a row, San Francisco lost to Dallas in the
NFC championship, this time by the score of 38–21.

Once again, Steve Young had to watch the Super

Bowl on television, just like millions of other people. He was a patient man, but he was growing weary of sitting on his couch and watching football in the last week of January.

At least he wasn't the only one quarterbacking from his living room. The Kansas City Chiefs lost the AFC championship game, so Joe Montana had to watch the game on television, too.

Chapter Eight
1994–1995

Champions at Last

Before the beginning of the 1994 season, Steve Young told one reporter, "Everything that has happened in my career has tried my patience more than I ever thought it would. It's made me see how much I can really take. . . . I've become a better human being because of leading teams, having struggles and successes."

Steve Young knew that despite his successes over the past few seasons, there was still a challenge that had eluded him: the Super Bowl. Until he led the 49ers to a win in the Super Bowl, neither he nor the team would be given the respect they felt they deserved.

Now, just as Steve's critics complained that he was not as tough or as good as Joe Montana, critics of the 49ers said the same things about the team when they compared them to Dallas. In order for Steve and the 49ers to even have a chance to silence their critics, they had to beat the Cowboys. Until they did, talk about the Super Bowl was just meaningless conversation.

In the off-season, the 49ers set out to build a team that could beat Dallas. Coach George Seifert was smart enough to know that it wasn't Steve Young's fault the 49ers had lost. Dallas just had better players. The 49er defense, in particular, couldn't seem to stop Troy Aikman, Emmitt Smith, or wide receiver Michael Irvin.

The team made one important improvement when they signed Dallas linebacker Ken Norton as a free agent. Not only did the move help San Francisco, but it also hurt the Cowboys. Then the 49ers acquired flamboyant defensive back and sometime baseball player Deion Sanders.

These additions solidified the 49er defense. At last, San Francisco's defense was as strong as its offense.

But when the season began, few people expected the 49ers to make it to their goal. The Cowboys still looked like the better team, and in the AFC, the

Kansas City Chiefs were favored to win. After all, they still had a quarterback named Joe Montana.

Montana had missed part of the 1993 season with some injuries, but when healthy, he was still effective. Everyone knew he was ready to retire and wanted to go to the Super Bowl one more time.

Just as Steve Young was determined to lead the 49ers out of the shadow of the Dallas Cowboys, he also personally hoped to emerge from the shadow of Joe Montana. He knew that unless he led the 49ers to a Super Bowl win, some San Francisco fans would still consider him to be second best.

Steve Young opened the season with a bang. Before a capacity crowd at Candlestick Park, he threw for over 300 yards and four touchdowns to lead the 49ers over the Los Angeles Raiders 44–14. It looked like another strong season for Steve Young and the 49ers.

But despite the big win, he was concerned. The 49ers' offensive line was banged up, and after all the off-season changes, the defense was still learning to play together. Steve wondered how the 49ers would play against a really good team.

He didn't have to wait long to find out. In the second game of the year, the 49ers traveled to Kansas City to play Joe Montana and the Chiefs.

In many people's minds, the matchup between Steve Young and Joe Montana was the biggest game of the year. Everyone knew that they hadn't really gotten along on the 49ers, that Steve had resented Joe just as Joe later resented Steve. Montana and the Chiefs wanted to use the game as a springboard to the league title. Kansas City owner Lamar Hunt even called the game "our championship in September."

Steve Young tried to downplay the situation, telling reporters, "It's a long season. We'll have to play fourteen games after this one, and we can't let this game make us lose our focus." Still, in the week before the game, sportswriters hyped the contest as if it were a fight between two boxers. Fans hoped to see a knockout. They wanted the game to answer the question everyone had been asking for years: "Who is the better quarterback, Young or Montana?"

They were disappointed in the result. Neither quarterback landed a knockout punch. Steve Young threw for more yardage and completed more of his passes than Joe Montana did, but he got knocked around by Kansas City's defensive line. Montana threw for two touchdowns and won the game, at 24–17.

Steve Young didn't avoid the press after the game or blame others for the loss. He took the blame and gave credit to Joe Montana and the Chiefs.

"Maybe the student still has something to learn from the master," he said. "Montana was great today. I've learned a lot of the game from him, and I don't have a problem admitting that." Steve knew this was only one game in a long season, and that one loss, even to Joe Montana, wouldn't kill the 49ers.

Over the next few weeks, San Francisco continued to struggle as the offensive line kept breaking down. Steve was still playing well, but he was under continual pressure from the attacking defense. San Francisco coaches worried that he might get hurt.

On October 2, the Philadelphia Eagles came to San Francisco. It didn't take long for the Eagles' powerful defensive line to start punching holes in the 49er offense. Steve Young took the brunt of Philadelphia's attack.

The 49er offense never got going. Each time Steve went back to pass, there was an Eagle in his face trying to knock him to the ground. Too often, he was forced to throw the ball too soon or throw it away. The 49ers failed to move and had to punt. The Eagles took advantage of good field position and punched the ball into the end zone.

Midway through the third quarter, with the Eagles up 33–8 and the 49ers facing a second-and-ten situation, Steve went back to pass. He knew that if the 49ers were going to come back and win, he had to throw the ball downfield.

Once again, the Eagles swarmed through the San Francisco line. Just as Steve released the ball, Eagle lineman William Fuller blasted into him, slamming him to the ground. The pass fell incomplete.

San Francisco coach George Seifert had seen enough. By his count, Steve had been hit hard nine or ten times already. Seifert considered the game out of reach and didn't want his starting quarterback to get hurt. He sent in second-string quarterback Elvis Grbac, who tapped Steve on the shoulder and told him to head to the sidelines.

Steve Young didn't want to be taken from the game. He still wanted to win.

When he got to the sidelines, the normally polite quarterback confronted Coach Seifert, demanding to know why he had been taken from the game. When Seifert told him, "We're afraid for you," Steve exploded. He began yelling at his coaches and didn't stop until he made sure everyone knew exactly what he thought of the decision. He even used a few words he had never used before.

Steve's teammates were shocked at his outburst. Fans watching from the stands were startled. Even Steve Young's parents, watching the game on television back in Greenwich, were stunned. "I had never seen him that . . . verbal," admitted Grit Young.

The 49ers went on to lose, 40–8, their worst defeat at home in more than twenty-five years. After the game, Steve Young refused to apologize. He explained why he hadn't wanted to come out of the game: "I don't even want to care about next week. I want today. . . . I want to finish everything I start.

I don't care how bad it is." The 49ers, he thought, had still had a chance to win.

It was Coach Seifert who apologized. He realized he should have talked to Steve before removing him and he shouldn't have taken him out in the middle of a series of plays.

The outburst seemed to spark the 49ers. A week later, down by two touchdowns to the Detroit Lions in the first quarter, Steve Young went back to pass. The Lions defense sprang forward after him.

Flushed out of the pocket, Steve rolled out toward the sideline. Instead of taking the easy way out and ducking out of bounds, he tried to gain the extra yard.

Three Lions had their sights set on the quarterback, and all three met him at the same time. Steve crumpled to the ground, and lay there for a moment, moaning. Then he dragged himself off the field and struggled to his feet. Elvis Grbac took his place.

Two plays later, Steve put himself back into the game.

In the huddle, his teammates saw a look of determination on his face they had never seen before. Steve

Young had meant what he said the week before, after the Philadelphia game. He wanted to win today.

The huddle broke, and the 49ers hustled to the line of scrimmage. Steve took the snap, faded to pass, and spotted Jerry Rice streaking down the sideline. The pass was perfect.

Lion defender Ryan McNeil had no choice but to wrap his arms around Rice to keep him from catching the ball. A pass interference penalty was better than a touchdown.

The penalty got the 49ers moving. Steve followed with a screen pass good for fifteen yards, then a short pass over the middle that went for twenty. Two plays later, the 49ers scored a touchdown. They went on to win, 27–21.

After that, Steve Young and the 49ers were almost unstoppable. Against Atlanta a week later, Steve completed his first 14 passes and 15 of 16 overall, for four touchdowns. The 49ers routed the Falcons 42–3. They rolled to two more victories in the following weeks. Then the Dallas Cowboys came to Candlestick Park.

The game meant little in the standings. Each team was securely ahead in its division. Players knew they would likely play each other in the NFC championship game. However, the winner of this matchup would have home field advantage in the playoffs.

It was a tough, physical game. Steve Young threw for two touchdowns and 183 yards. He ran for sixty yards more and a third score. San Francisco won, 21–14.

The 49ers stormed through the remainder of the regular season, to finish 14–2. It was the best season of Steve Young's career. Over the last six games of the season, he threw for a total of 17 touchdowns with only two interceptions.

No one in the history of the National Football League, not even Joe Montana, had ever played the position better. His quarterback rating was 112.8, an all-time single season record, while his career rating of 96.8 was the best in NFL history — just ahead of Joe Montana — as was his career completion record of 63.6 percent. His 35 touchdown passes and 70.2 percent completion mark set new 49er standards, breaking records previously held by Montana. Steve Young was named Player of the Week twice, Player of the Month once, and NFL Player of the Year.

But that was yesterday. As the 49ers entered the

playoffs, Steve Young knew that unless San Francisco made it to the Super Bowl, all those individual awards would mean nothing. When fans started talking about quarterbacks, they'd always mention Joe Montana first.

San Francisco destroyed the Chicago Bears 44–15 in the first round of the playoffs, while the Cowboys similarly demolished Green Bay, winning 35–9. As predicted, it was to be a 49ers-Cowboys rematch for the NFC championship. In the minds of many, the NFC championship game, and not the Super Bowl, would be the game that matched the two best teams in the NFL.

The week before the game, it rained so hard in San Francisco that the 49ers traveled to Arizona in order to be able to practice in dry weather.

Each team wanted to win badly. The Cowboys were hungry for their third consecutive Super Bowl, while the 49ers hoped for a chance to prove themselves. All week long, players from each team badmouthed each other in the newspapers. When game day finally arrived, the adrenaline was running wild.

Candlestick Park was already packed to capacity when the two teams charged out onto the field for pregame warm-ups. Almost immediately, the players began jostling and pushing each other.

Such behavior was expected from the flamboyant Cowboys, but the 49ers had always been more reserved. But after losing to Dallas two years in a row, the 49ers had decided to play Dallas's game. Instead of being intimidated, they were going to do the intimidating.

Although it had stopped raining, the field was a quagmire. Both teams knew that it would be important to get off to a quick start before the field became too sloppy.

Steve Young knew he had to play well. But he also knew he couldn't try to win the game totally by himself. He had to be patient and aggressive at the same time.

Before the game, he told a reporter that he felt it was "imperative that we win the championship." Although he admitted that he regretted losing to Dallas the past two seasons, he added that "It doesn't weigh on me personally. It weighs on me as part of this team." He didn't want to win because of what a win could do for Steve Young. He wanted to win because of the opportunity it provided the San Francisco 49ers.

The 49ers lost the coin toss, and Dallas elected to receive. The Cowboys started off aggressively. On the third play of the game, Dallas quarterback Troy Aikman dropped back and spotted wide receiver Kevin Williams wide open. He rifled the ball in his direction.

But 49er cornerback Eric Davis was watching closely. Although he was supposed to help cover Michael Irvin, the Cowboys' other receiver, when he saw Aikman look toward Williams, he left Irvin and cut toward Williams.

Williams reached out for the ball, but it never got there. Davis cut in front of him for the interception and saw nothing but open space ahead. He raced 44 yards for a touchdown! The 49ers led, 7–0.

Once again, San Francisco kicked off to Dallas. Now the Cowboys were even more anxious to score.

On the third play of the series, Aikman dropped back to make another pass. Michael Irvin was open.

This time the receiver caught the ball. But as Irvin turned upfield, there was Eric Davis again. He hit Irvin hard and pulled the ball loose.

A herd of Cowboys and 49ers pounced on the ball

at the Dallas 39-yard line. Then the referees started signaling toward the 49er goal.

San Francisco's ball! All sixty-nine thousand fans in Candlestick Park stood and roared!

Steve Young trotted out onto the field, determined to take advantage of the fumble and get a touchdown.

San Francisco tried a few running plays before calling a pass. Steve looked out at the Dallas defense, but he wasn't worried about the Cowboys' rush. His offensive linemen had all recovered from their earlier injuries.

Steve barked out the signals, took the ball from the center, and skipped back a few steps while he looked downfield. Then he spotted running back Ricky Watters breaking free over the middle.

It was a classic 49er play. While the defense worried about Jerry Rice and John Taylor on the outside, the 49ers ran running backs and the tight end over the middle, which was usually left open. Steve's pass hit Watters on the run. He cut between defenders to the end zone. Touchdown! San Francisco now led 14–0.

For the third time in less than five minutes, the 49ers kicked off. The Cowboys' Kevin Williams took the ball on the fly and started upfield, but was hit by the 49ers' Adam Walker. The ball popped loose again!

Another mad scramble yielded the same result. San Francisco's ball!

Steve didn't waste time. He smartly moved the 49ers upfield, playing it safe with the two-touchdown lead. With the ball on the one-yard line, fullback William Floyd bulled his way into the end zone. Only six minutes and 33 seconds into the game, the 49ers led 21–0!

But the Cowboys didn't quit. Just before the end of the quarter, Aikman hit Irvin on a 44-yard touchdown pass to make the score 21–7. In the second quarter, San Francisco followed with a field goal, but the Cowboys marched the length of the field and Emmitt Smith ran in for a touchdown. San Francisco now led by only ten points, 24–14.

Just before halftime, the 49ers were forced to punt. Dallas took over at their 16-yard line with only a minute left to play.

Dallas coach Barry Switzer had confidence in his

team. Instead of trying to run out the clock, he decided to try for another score.

Aikman went back to pass on three straight downs. Each time the 49er defense forced him to make a bad pass or throw the ball away. Now Dallas had to punt.

The kick was short, and the 49ers took over at the Dallas 39-yard line, just out of field goal range. With only a few seconds left in the half and his team ahead by ten points, everyone expected Steve Young to either take the snap and down the ball or throw a quick sideline pass in an effort to get in field goal range and stop the clock. In the stands, some fans left their seats to get something to eat or drink during halftime.

Those who did missed the play of the game. Steve and the 49er coaches figured the Cowboys wouldn't expect San Francisco to try to score a touchdown. This was no time to be patient.

Steve stood behind the center again and called out the signals. As he looked over the Cowboy defense, he saw that the cornerbacks and safeties were playing tight. They were expecting the sideline pass. He knew exactly what to do. So did Jerry Rice.

The center snapped the ball, and Steve took three quick steps back. Then he lofted a pass toward the back left corner of the end zone.

On the left side, Rice broke from the line of scrimmage and drove right past the startled Dallas defender, who immediately turned and gave chase.

As Rice reached the end zone, he turned and looked over his right shoulder.

Outlined against the blue sky, he saw the ball spiraling down over his head.

He jumped, stretched out his arms, and reached for the ball.

It landed right in his hands as he tumbled into the end zone.

Touchdown!

Steve Young danced his way toward Jerry Rice and joined his teammates in celebration. The surprise play had worked! Jerry Rice had run a perfect pass route, and Steve Young had thrown a perfect pass at the perfect time. As the 49ers and Cowboys ran off the field at halftime a few moments later, San Francisco led 31–14.

The Cowboys were stunned. The last-second touchdown broke their spirit.

The game was all but over. Although the Cowboys scored two second-half touchdowns, Steve Young put the game out of reach when he scored a touchdown on a three-yard keeper. The 49ers won, 38–28.

As soon as the game ended, Steve took off his helmet and ran to the side of the field, where he spotted Grit and Sherry Young sitting in the stands. A huge grin broke out on his face. He waved at his parents, happier than he had been in a long, long time.

The fans sitting around the Youngs saw Steve wave and started cheering and waving back at him. Then the fans sitting next to them did the same thing. Soon, the whole crowd was standing and waving and cheering Steve Young.

He couldn't believe his eyes. He wanted to thank everyone for standing behind him. He broke into a slow trot and ran around the entire field, slapping hands with the fans, accepting their congratulations, and saying "thanks" over and over again. He finally belonged. The shadow of the Dallas Cowboys was gone, and that of Joe Montana was growing dim. As Steve Young circled the field in the bright California sun, there was no doubt in anyone's mind that he was the 49er quarterback. Statistically it had been one of Steve Young's least impressive games, as he completed only 13 of 29 passes for 159 yards. But those 159 yards had been plenty.

They were enough to take the 49ers all the way across the country, from San Francisco to Joe Robbie Stadium in Miami, Florida.

That's where Super Bowl XXIX was being played.

Chapter Nine
1995

A Super Super Bowl

Before the Super Bowl, Steve Young had never felt so confident. Not only did he have a chance to fulfill his dream, but another Super Bowl win for the 49ers would be the team's fifth, the most won by any single team in NFL history. That sounded good to Steve. He decided he didn't just want to win, he wanted to make history.

In order to do so, the 49ers would have to defeat the AFC champion San Diego Chargers. The Chargers were a tough, physical football team. Their defense, led by linebacker Junior Seau, had been one of the best in pro football during the 1994 season. On offense, quarterback Stan Humphries had had the best season of his career, while running back Natrone Means always seemed to get the tough yardage when they needed it. The Chargers were no pushovers. The 49ers would have to play their best game of the year.

In practice the week before the game, the 49ers tried to stay focused and not get too confident. In the locker room each day, 49er offensive lineman Harris Barton walked up to Steve Young and started brushing his back. "Got to get that monkey off your back, Steve," he said. Steve would just look at the big lineman and smile. He knew Barton was trying to keep him loose and was simply reminding him that the Super Bowl was his chance to shine.

The day of the game, the 49ers were big favorites, a dangerous situation for San Francisco. It gave the underdog Chargers plenty of motivation and left the 49ers open to criticism if they failed to win big. The players all knew that a close win wouldn't satisfy everyone.

Just before the game started, there was a big celebration on the field, with bands, music, singing, and fireworks. At the conclusion of the show, the players were introduced and ran out on the field. Steve Young was ready.

He went out to the center of the field with the other captains for the coin toss. The 49ers won and elected to receive the ball. Steve Young hoped his team's good luck would hold up.

As smoke from the fireworks lingered over the field, the Chargers kicked the ball deep downfield.

The 49ers' Derrick Carter caught the ball on the 17-yard line and raced upfield. The Chargers swarmed over him at the 29. As he went down, an official tossed a yellow flag in the air.

"Face mask, San Diego," he called out, and signaled. "Fifteen-yard penalty. First down, San Francisco!" The 49ers' offense took the field. So far, everything was going their way.

As Steve Young ran out onto the field, the cheers of the crowd grew faint in his ears. Once the game began, he rarely heard the fans. He just concentrated on what he had to do.

The 49ers usually begin each game with a "script." Steve and his coaches sit down and select the first ten or fifteen plays they plan to use. Although Young has the right to "audibilize," or change the play, the 49ers usually try to stick to the script. They use it to set up the defense for certain plays.

When Steve reached the huddle, he stuck right to the script. On the first play, William Floyd bulled into the middle of the line for four yards. On second-down-and-six, Steve faded back to pass and hit John Taylor over the middle for eleven yards and a first down on the San Diego 44-yard line.

Everyone on the 49er offense knew what play the script called for next. But when the 49ers met in the huddle, Harris Barton looked at Steve and said, "You've got to audibilize. You can't see anything through the smoke."

Steve glanced up, then looked downfield. There was still a lot of fireworks smoke in the air. But he knew that the Chargers couldn't see through the smoke any better than the 49ers could. Besides, the Chargers had surprised the 49ers by using a defense they hadn't been prepared for. Steve wasn't quite sure what to change the play to.

"We'll stick to the script," he said. Then he called the play, a pass to Jerry Rice over the middle of the field.

The 49ers broke from the huddle. Steve Young crouched behind the center and surveyed the San Diego defense. It looked as if they had the play stopped cold. Two defensive backs were certain to be covering Jerry Rice.

For a moment, Steve thought about changing the play again, then decided not to. If I wait long enough, he thought, Jerry still should be able to get open for half a second. If I throw a perfect pass . . .

Steve called out the signals. The center snapped the ball.

To Steve Young, everything seemed to take place in slow motion. As he retreated in the pocket, he watched Jerry Rice throw a few fakes at a defender and start his pass route. Then Steve noticed the pocket forming around him as his offensive linemen fought to keep the Chargers at bay.

Rice broke across the middle and turned upfield, but Steve waited. He had to be patient. If he threw the ball too soon, the defender would be able to cut the ball off.

Then he saw Rice start to break free. Actually, he wasn't even free yet, but Steve knew that by the time the ball got there, Rice would take a few more steps and be between defenders. Steve let the pass fly.

It spun in a perfect spiral just over the huge hand of a San Diego lineman and on downfield. Jerry Rice, eyes wide open, reached out to catch the ball.

One defender reached out to knock the ball down. He missed it by inches.

The other defender closed on Rice. He, too, tried to knock the ball down.

Jerry Rice kept his eyes on the ball. It landed as soft as a feather in his hands.

He turned upfield. Both tacklers reached out for him, but Jerry Rice was gone.

Touchdown! The 49ers led, 7–0! Steve Young had thrown the pass at just the right instant. His patience had paid off again!

San Francisco didn't start celebrating. The players just looked at each other and slapped hands. They knew there was still a long way to go in the game.

The 49ers kicked off, and San Diego took over. Three plays later, the 49er defense forced them to punt. San Francisco took over at their own 21-yard line.

Steve Young stuck to the script. First Ricky Watters ran up the middle. Then Steve threw to Floyd in the flat for a short gain. It was third down.

The script called for another pass, but as Steve dropped back in the pocket, a Charger lineman broke free. Steve pulled the ball down and started to run.

Even though he was thirty-three years old, Steve was still one of the best running quarterbacks in the game. He scrambled for a 21-yard gain down the right sidelines before being pushed out of bounds.

When a quarterback can scramble, it slows the defense down. The linebackers sometimes hesitate just a half-second to make sure the quarterback isn't running the ball before they go to cover the receivers.

That's just what happened next. According to the script, the 49ers had selected the perfect play, a pass to running back Ricky Watters in the middle of the field.

Steve took the ball from center and dropped back to pass again. Watters pretended to throw a block, then circled toward the center of the field.

Steve looked downfield. He saw the San Diego linebacker who was supposed to cover Watters hesitate, making sure the quarterback wasn't being flushed from the pocket.

That's all Steve Young needed. Rice and Taylor had pulled the rest of the secondary to the sideline. Steve threw a bullet to Watters.

Watters caught the ball running at full speed. The San Diego linebacker was too late.

No one could catch the speedy running back. He raced into the end zone for another San Francisco touchdown, bringing the score to 14–0, 49ers!

The Chargers regrouped. After taking the kickoff, they used sixteen plays to march 78 yards downfield, with Natrone Means going over from the one-yard line to make the score 14–7.

All that did was slow the 49ers down. When they got the ball back, Steve Young resumed his assault on the San Diego defense.

The Chargers didn't know what to do. When they looked for one play, the 49ers used another. When they had the right defense, it didn't seem to matter; Steve Young completed the pass anyway.

He drove his team down the field in textbook fashion. After starting on the 49er 30-yard line, Young threw to Rice over the middle for a 19-yard gain.

The series of passes over the middle were all designed to set the Chargers up for the next play. While San Diego looked inside, Rice circled around from the end and took a handoff from Young on a reverse. The play was good for ten yards. The 49ers were on the move.

After an incomplete pass, a throw to Taylor

gained 12. Then a run, a quarterback scramble for 15 yards, a pass to Rice on the sideline, and a defensive penalty brought the 49ers inside the ten-yard line.

Three plays later, Steve pitched the ball to Floyd in the end zone for his third touchdown pass. The lead was back to 14 points in San Francisco's favor.

The Chargers were helpless. Midway through the second quarter, the 49er defense shut down San Diego and the 49ers took over at midfield.

Steve almost made it look too easy. On the ninth play of the drive, he zipped the ball to Watters in the end zone.

Four touchdown passes for Steve Young! Twenty-eight points for San Francisco!

San Diego managed to kick a field goal, and the two teams left the field at halftime with San Francisco leading, 28–10.

Yet in the locker room, the 49ers were not celebrating. An 18-point lead was good, but after scoring 44 points against the Bears in the playoffs, then 38 points against the Cowboys in the NFC championship game, the 49ers knew they could win big. To do that, they had to remain focused the entire game. They wanted the world to know they were the best team in pro football.

It didn't take them long to prove it in the second half. San Diego took the kickoff but failed to move the ball and had to punt again. The 49ers got the ball on their own 38. Four minutes and eight seconds later, Ricky Watters scored on a nine-yard run, bringing the tally up to 35–10 San Francisco.

That still wasn't enough. Before the quarter ended, San Francisco scored again, this time on Steve Young's fifth touchdown pass, again to Jerry Rice. The 49ers now led 42–10.

San Diego returned the kickoff for a touchdown, then added a two-point conversion to make the score 42–18, but the 49ers weren't finished.

The two teams exchanged punts, then the 49ers took over on the San Diego 32-yard line with only eights seconds left in the third quarter. Steve Young trotted onto the field.

Five years before, he had stood on the sidelines watching as Joe Montana threw for a Super Bowl–record five touchdowns in the 49ers' 55–10 rout of Denver. Steve had already tied Montana's mark with five touchdown passes of his own. Now he wanted the record for himself.

It took Ricky Watters three carries to get the 49ers to the seven-yard line. The 49ers' script was over. Steve called the play.

He dropped back quickly and looked over the middle to Jerry Rice. The wide receiver had made his job easy all year, getting open and making big catches game after game. Steve wanted to break the record while throwing to his favorite target.

Rice slanted across the goal line. Steve threw a line drive.

Rice gathered the ball into his arms, held it for a moment, then threw his hands in the air.

Touchdown!

Steve Young punched his fist in the air and joined his teammates in the end zone. The touchdown pass record was his, and the 49ers led, 49–18.

When the 49ers got the ball back, Steve returned to the field. He felt so good, he wanted to play forever. But his teammates finally convinced him he had done enough, and he left the field midway through the fourth quarter to let Elvis Grbac take his place.

From every corner of Joe Robbie Stadium, the fans stood and cheered for Steve Young as he trotted off the field. Now he could hear them, and he stood with his helmet in his hand, hugging his teammates and enjoying the moment. He had waited a long, long time for this.

San Diego scored a meaningless touchdown late, and Super Bowl XXIX ended with a final score of San Francisco 49, San Diego 26. The 49ers were world champions!

In the locker room after the game, the 49ers whooped and hollered and sprayed each other with champagne. Even Steve Young got soaked. He didn't want to drink any, but he didn't mind how it felt dripping down his back. There was no "monkey" to stop it. In the biggest game of his life, he had completed 24 of 36 passes for 325 yards and six touchdowns.

Reporters crowded around Steve and peppered him with questions. How did it feel to win? Did he know he was selected as the Super Bowl MVP? Had he finally emerged from Joe Montana's shadow?

Young just grinned in the spotlight cast by the television cameras. He didn't see any shadows anymore. He tried to answer their questions as best as he could.

"I wish everyone who ever played football could feel this," he said. "This was the big game. We had to face the Cowboys, then win this game, and we did everything we had to do to stand out as the best."

At his own locker nearby, Ricky Watters concurred. "You couldn't have written a better script for Steve Young to come out and play just a flawless, I mean a flawless, game," he said. Steve just smiled.

Then a reporter asked Steve Young if he had anything to say to his critics, the people who hadn't thought he was good enough to win the Super Bowl.

Young's grin grew broader. "The heck with them," he said. "They can go bother somebody else for a while."

Then he added, "This was my best effort, but I hope there will be more to come."

The patient man was already looking ahead, though for the moment, he was content. "I wish every player who ever played in the NFL could feel what I feel right now," he added. "It's so incredible after all I've gone through to finally be on the mountaintop looking down."

Matt Christopher

Michael Jordan

Steve Young

Wayne Gretzky

Grant Hill